CLAN

I

UNIF

"DAH- -OO- ME?"
"N"

# CLANGERS in UNIFORM

compiled by
Lieut Colonel R. J. Dickinson
and
Bill Hooper

m

Published by
Midas Books
12 Dene Way, Speldhurst,
Tunbridge Wells, Kent.

## CLANGERS

Being a collection of blunders, boobs, botches, bloomers, bon mots, quips, muck-ups – of sending-up and puttings-down, which are reported as happening in the fighting services.


## ACKNOWLEDGEMENTS

The acknowledgements of the compilers are due to all those, who wittingly or unwittingly contributed material for this book. Their names, even if known, would be too numerous to list here, but mention must be made of Commander A.B. Campbell RN (Rtd) who provided some recollections of naval occasions and of Mr Charles A. Fox of the Artists Rifles who recalled so many army actions. No doubt Lieut-Commander 'Dan' Bylge-Cox RNVR, Major-General C.O. Littlewart and P.O. Percy Prune would be deeply offended if they were omitted from the list so they duly receive a mention as representing all the unknown warriors who have happily boobed and clanged their way through their service lives.

NOT GETTING THE
USUAL PEACETIME
RECRUIT
"OH - HE WROTE IT!"
"AWRIGHT, I'LL DEAL WITH YOU -
LATER MILTON!"
"AIRMAN!"
SPROGS' HELL
PADGATE
PARADE GROUND

THAT NOTORIOUS BATTLEFIELD
– BLACKPOOL
"NAH! I MEAN A REAL SERGEANT!"
"...THEY HAD TWO BLOODY ENEMIES..."
"WHO D'YE THINK THEY HIT FIRST?"
RAF SP
LOOK AROUND YOU
THE HUN IS ALWAYS
ID
YOU
Love Tooty
"CAREL
TALK
COST
VES

ISBN 0 85936 036 9

To be published in the same series Clangers in the House, Clangers in Law, Clangers in Print and Clangers at the Bar.

Printed in Great Britain by
Lewis Reprints Ltd.,
member of Brown Knight & Truscott Group
London and Tonbridge.

# Introduction

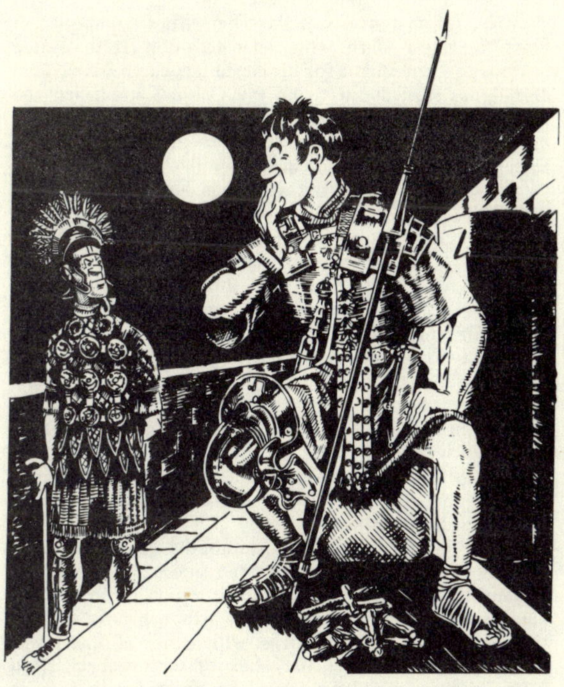

In peace and war, from the dim past to the present day, men in armies, navies and in recent – historically speaking – times, air forces have been the creators or the victims of the faux pas enumerated in the title of this book and have found themselves in the brig, doing jankers or, in RAF terms, shot down in flames – or if they are lucky just reprimanded. The compilers of this collection dare claim that most of the anecdotes that follow are true although they must admit that the settings of all the stories cannot be meticulously confirmed, since classic examples have been told and re-told over so many years that their sources cannot always be traced.

Who, for instance, can say where the yarn about the sentry on night guard, who called to a dim figure passing near his post for a light for his illegal fag, came from? That dim figure turned out to be the Colonel and when the petrified sentry apologised his C.O. said 'That's all right, but take care, I could have been a second-lieutenant and then you would have been in real trouble'.

In various forms, that yarn has been set in South Africa in the Boer War, in Flanders in the first World War and has cropped up again in North Africa, France, Germany – in fact in any theatre of war and has been told as having happened in all three services and even, according to one issue of an army magazine, in the American army in the Pacific theatre.

Who is to say whether or not it had its origin in early Britain when a Roman soldier may have unthinkingly asked his centurion for the loan of his flint to make a warning fire against Hadrian's Wall?– or in the Peninsular campaign when a humble private may have dropped his clanger by asking old Nosey for a light for his clay pipe? The fact that it was still being told within living memory illustrates the fact that a funny story never dates even though the date of its birth cannot be surely certified.

Anyway, men who have seen action are prone to remember only the funny things which were said or happened – amusing incidents which are only slightly tinged with the bloody horror, which they all know war really is, so that, when they talk of their war, it often seems to those who have never been under fire that it was all a bit of a lark. That last fact may have prompted the remark made by a cockney lady, who, at the height of the London blitz, was being helped out of the ruins of her home in the East end and on being asked where her husband was, recalling some of his oft-times told tales of his army experiences said 'Oh, him! 'E's in the army – cowardly sod!'

In lighter vein, as a more peaceful introduction to this little book of service anecdotes and clangers it may not be inappropriate to quote the words of welcome used by a

*"Welcome to my H.Q. my boy"*

senior officer – wrongly identified by some as Major-General 'Clanger' Littlewart himself* – when welcoming a young officer to his HQ. 'Welcome to my HQ my boy,' he said. 'Do not think that this is one of those HQ where all the work is done by half the chaps and the rest just loaf around doing nothing – oh no, its quite the reverse!' The young officer caught his drift all right and soon proved to himself the truth of the music hall joke that whilst bread was the staff of life, life on the staff was not one big loaf. But he was a career soldier and had to lump it, for it must be remembered that there are all sorts of soldiers – some are born soldiers, others become soldiers and others have soldiering thrust upon them. That goes for the other services too of course. Not all those who find themselves suddenly thrust into uniform entirely appreciate the gesture, as the tales that immediately follow serve to show.

---

* See 'Officers' Mess' – Midas Books, 12 Dene Way, Speldhurst, Tunbridge Wells, Kent.

"YOU'LL BE SORRY!"
"..... 'E'S IN THE ARMY COWARDLY SOD"
"ALL BLEEDIN' DAY"
"BLOODY FIRM BELONGS TO ME!"
"BLOODY AIN'T WITH THE AIR FORCE"
DAILY H
"...'UTS AND MANTLE 'EM AGAIN"
BILL HOOPER

# I.
# YOU'LL BE SORRY.

He was everything an airman should not be. His uniform, just issued, was a sloppy affair; his cap was set on an untidy mop of hair, dead straight; his brasses were a dull orange colour and his dirty boots had, both left and right, laces trailing. His ill-tied tie was well over to starboard, one wing of his collar stuck up under his chin and both breast pocket buttons were undone. He slouched over a patch of green sward, tripping over the little notice 'KEEP OFF THE GRASS', but what incensed the Flight-Sergeant more than anything was the unlit fag which drooped from the horrible man's slack mouth. 'AIRMAN! CUMM'ERE!' yelled Chiefy. The idle one tooled over to stand slackly in front of the immaculate NCO. 'How long have you been in the Royal Air Force?' asked Flight acidly. The scruffy sprog sighed deeply and there was a tremor in his voice as he said 'All bleedin' day'.

Nicholas on the other hand was a recruiting Sergeant's dream come true. He was born in Scandinavia where his father had been a British Consul and had married a Swedish lady. Nicholas had come to Britain to volunteer to fight for the country of his father's birth, but, although he'd tried everything, he couldn't 'get in'. He put it down to the accent he then had which to the uninitiated could, he says, have sounded 'Cherman'.

He took an office job in the City and one day, during the lunch hour, he was walking past Lloyds when he saw posters inviting young men to join the London Scottish Regiment. Nick was impressed by the two tall pipers flanking the entrance, dressed in kilts of Hodden Grey. Well, he'd tried everything else and so in he went to the rooms, which Lloyds had set aside for recruiting, to try his luck with the London Scottish. He was greeted by a tall Highlander who looked with approval at this equally tall and fit-looking applicant. The Sergeant asked a few initial questions, but, like others before him, was obviously puzzled by Nick's accent. 'Wheer d'ye come fra' laddie?' he asked in a kindly fashion. 'Scandinaviah' replied Nicholas. The Sergeant walked to a window and looked out for a moment or two and then, appearing to have made up his mind, he returned to the table and wrote something on Nick's application. Rolling his tongue around inside his cheek he gave Nick a broad wink. 'Shetlands' he said flatly. 'You're *in* laddie.'

Two weeks later Nicholas was happily undergoing his square bashing – kilted like the rest – a happy Viking from the Shetlands.

Alfie was like our first 'volunteer' – a disgruntled misfit, conscripted according to his age group, but not mustered in the trade he wanted. A craftsman in 'civvy street', he had been given menial tasks ever since being called up. He'd been chivvied by NCOs till he thought he'd go mad and now, on leave, his mother was having friends to tea to show him off. 'Ooh,' said one lady as she came into the front room, 'Look, Alfie's with the RAF.' 'Bloody ain't *with* the Air Force', remarked this gallant boy in blue, 'Been *against* 'em since they bloody got me.'

It may not be possible at this stage to confirm the story which is told against the dismal winter backdrop of the barbed wire and huts of RAF Padgate, 1939. One of that 'thick' breed of NCO told off a squad of airmen-under-training to go back to the ''uts' they'd been occupying since arrival and dismantle their beds. 'Then' he added, 'take 'em over to those 'uts and mantle 'em again.'

The regulars as well as the early volunteers among the ground crews of the RAF were sometimes exasperated by the 'binding' of lately joined conscripts. Those who, it was said, had been dragged up the road screaming, could be a bore to those who had seen some service – voluntarily. But one conscript had a degree of excuse. 'Fifteen blokes in the firm were deferred' he grumbled. 'Fifteen – because of their essential war work – and three others including me, were called up.' A hoary veteran of a couple of years' war service said 'Well – ain't you the lucky one mate!' 'I don't think so' replied the disgruntled one, 'bloody firm belongs to me!'

Throughout the army – in fact the world – the Ghurkhas have a reputation for the reverse of 'dodging the column' if there's a tough job to be done. Accordingly it came as a distinct surprise when no volunteers were forthcoming from a certain unit to train as parachutists. The battalion was on parade; the officer had explained the requirement and had asked all those who would volunteer to take a pace forward. No one had moved. The officer repeated the 'recruiting speech' explaining 'you'll be taken up in an aeroplane; then you'll jump and when you land – probably behind the enemy lines – you will have the time of your lives chopping their heads off with your kukris'. The Ghurkhas grinned and nudged each other gleefully at such a jolly prospect but, although there was some shuffling, no one stepped forward. Then light dawned on the officer. 'You will, of course,' he added, 'have parachutes.'

As a man the whole battalion took a pace forward.

Once the unhappy conscript has joined the forces, his volunteering days really begin. 'I want three volunteers – you, you and you.' This time honoured approach to pressganging in the army was varied by a certain sergeant instructor at the OCTU at Shorncliffe in 1939. He used to enter a hut and start 'Is there any *cay*det...?' and any caydet who was not obviously gainfully employed was led away to shovel snow, of which there was plenty, or to some other such attractive occupation. This sergeant was very mean in the American sense of the word for he would sometimes enter the hut and say 'Is there any caydet... (awesome pause as the surprised cadets frantically sought cover) who' he continued, 'would like to go into Folkestone as there's a lorry outside that's just leaving.' Glad stampede. By this artful double dealing he was never short of volunteers.

Strangely enough not all volunteers are welcomed – especially those who are late for the parade or function for which they have volunteered. Listen how RSM Bowles of the Grenadier Guards dealt with such a volunteer. 'Trooper Piper', he opened patiently, 'I didn't make you come 'ere; I didn't order you to come 'ere; I didn't force you, you volunteered and now that you are 'ere (voice rising to the climax) why are you such a voluntary ..... nuisance?'

Why indeed? The old army maxim still holds good – never volunteer for anything. If you do – you'll be sorry!

# II.
# 'AIR CUT YOU.

The favourite prey of regimental police and Red Caps is the untidy and ill-dressed serviceman – particularly the ones with long hair. The hair of the head was expected to be kept short, but not necessarily crew cut. Nowadays the hair can be worn without fear at a length which, in the old days, would have sent the wearer straight to the Guard Room or at least would have earned a severe reprimand from the RSM and the promise, in no polite terms, of dire punishment if it were not properly cut by the next parade. The tale is told of an old type RSM who was impatiently waiting his turn in the barber's shop whilst the 'hair stylist' dealt with the youthful occupant of the chair, trimming every wave with loving care, curling, setting and spraying to his exact taste. At long last he was done and the RSM took his seat. To the enquiry how would he like it done, he replied brusquely, 'Same as yesterday'.

Beards are fairly commonplace in the Royal Navy but permission has still to be requested to grow one or rather 'not to shave'. In the Army by tradition the only man allowed to grow a beard is the Pioneer Sergeant, Queen Victoria forbade the growing of moustaches in the Navy out of respect for the Prince Consort on his death but they flourish luxuriantly in the Army and Royal Air Force, in fact Charlie Chaplin moustaches are definitely not allowed: it has to be a proper job or nothing. In the RAF this led to disciplinary action on one occasion.

The 'Plumber' hated the airman. The airman worked as a mechanic at a bench in the hangar and the 'Plumber' or more properly, the Engineer Officer was his supreme boss. Apart from a quite startling facial feature the airman was a rather insignificant chap – though a very efficient worker. The facial feature was the most luxurious and sweeping moustache, dark brown in colour. It offended the 'Plumber' and on his frequent tours of the workshops and hangars he eyed that glorious 'tash' with obvious detestation. The 'Plumber' himself had tried so hard to raise a moustache but so far, after several months, all he'd achieved was a thin crop of bum-fluff on his port side and some pathetic tendrils to starboard.*

The 'Plumber' developed something of a neurosis over the airman's moustache and one day went so far as to tell the erk's flight-sergeant to tell him 'to trim that thing – tidy himself up'. But the little airman's 'tash' continued to flourish.

The Engineer Officer's obsession led him to have the airman put on a charge. Over at the flights, where this had become something of a family joke, it was suggested that the charge might be framed as 'being in improper possession of a Group-Captain's moustache'. When the airman came before his CO he was told shortly to have his 'tash' trimmed. The airman flatly, though respectfully, refused and when asked upon what grounds he refused the order he appealed to the Warrant Officer present for a copy of King's Regulations. Deftly he turned up the appropriate section and showed it to the officer. It ran 'Beards and whiskers will not be worn; if a moustache is worn, the upper lip shall be entirely unshaven'. (Or words to that effect.) No case. The Engineer Officer kerfuffled a bit about 'keeping smart even though doing a dirty job sometimes....' but he had been shot down in flames and the erk went back to his bench in his pristine hirsute glory whilst the 'Plumber' went to his quarters, committed hari-kari on his futile hirsutage and appeared next day as glabrous as any Roman centurion.

Even in wartime a reasonable standard of smartness of the uniform is expected. In fact, the Battle of Britain was fought by pilots wearing their best blue – the same pattern of uniform as that in which they 'walked out' – battle dress was not introduced until later. When it was, commissioned pilots wore it as often as possible to save their 'best blue' for special occasions. At one special or

---

*Sometimes known as a 'soccertash' (eleven a side).

semi-special occasion in the Mess a pilot was approached by his CO who considered that he was rather overdoing the casual, sloppy PO Prune bit. 'Couldn't you have smartened yourself up a bit?' he asked. 'But sir,' replied the PO, 'you said best blue would be worn'. The Squadron Leader eyed the PO's rumpled 'best blue' and said 'Not *that* worn!'.

A certain airman took special steps to see that he looked his best in blue. He was of the type later to be known as a spiv. By dint of bribing the Stores wallah he contrived to acquire a spare uniform which he managed to send off to a tailor friend in 'Sarf Lundon' to have the trousers widened, the shoulders padded and the waist basted to fit tightly. The first time he went off camp in his new and illegally altered uniform he felt a treat and thought he looked it but in the Guard Room he couldn't leave well alone. He said to the service policeman in charge ''Ow do I look Corp?' The s.p. looked him up and down closely and then walked round him. 'Well,' he remarked, 'I suppose you look alright but you're not going out on pass like that. Not unless' he added, 'you go backwards.' 'Backwards?' exclaimed the dandy. 'Yes, backwards – you've got your cap on back to front.' Indeed his badge was at the back right instead of front left and he was sent out of the Guard Room to walk to his billet – backwards.

Even in North Africa the soldier could still take a pride in his appearance. Those suede 'chukka boots' – a bit like jodhpur boots were de rigueur among the doggier type of officer in the desert campaigns. Familiarly known as 'brothel creepers', in London shops they came to be known by the trade as 'Desert Boots'. A certain young officer fancied a pair, ordered them and in due course proudly wore them 'round the town'. They soon became a bit grubby so he gave them to his Arab servant – inevitably Ali – to clean. All ready to tool down to the nearest bar he called to Ali 'Haven't you finished my boots yet?' Back came the reply, 'Not long now sir, shine just coming.'

Officers' batmen often used to help themselves from their officer's wardrobe if they wanted to tart themselves up specially for some reason but this batman might more appropriately have raided a WAAF officer's quarter because, not to put too fine a point on it, he was precious. He was careful to confine his fairy ways to his off-duty hours but those who had seen him in some bar during these times, giggling with kindred queens, knew him to be 'as ginger as a tom cat'. He was waiting one evening in the corridor of the Guard Room as an RAF Service Policeman looked over his pass. He was in civvies, dressed in a figure hugging light check suit, violet shirt, yellow tie and green suedes. He exuded a delicate odour of sweet violets.

An airman from the flights came in – due for a 'forty-eight' and as smartly turned out as only those airmen who usually do a dirty job know how to look. Uniform meticulously pressed and brasses brilliant. He was a beefy bloke and had trouble getting past the batman in the narrow passage and got a good whiff of those sweet violets. He paused and looked the other up and down and then said, quite amiably, 'You ought to be wearing f.....g ear-rings.'

The exquisite appeared shocked – 'What!' he bleated, 'with tweeds?'

Apparel oft proclaims the man, so Shakespeare said, but often the observer refuses deliberately to accept the evidence of his eyes. This is an old tale of two enemies but can stand the repetition. They had detested each other at school and later at university but had masochistically followed each other's careers over the decades since. Now, in war-time, as a bishop and an admiral, they caught each other's eye on Platform 1 at Paddington. The Bishop, a portly figure, gaitered and aproned, walked slowly over to the Admiral. To the gorgeously gold braided and be-ribboned sailor he breathed, 'Do tell me porter, does the two-forty five for Reading go from this platform?' The 'sea-lord's' complexion took on a pucer shade but he replied quite civilly whilst gazing down at the gaiters and skirt-like apron, 'I think you will find that it goes from Platform 3, *Madam,* but in your condition I should have thought it would be dangerous to travel.'

Servicemen are frequently put in the book or 'on the

hooks' for being improperly dressed but it is not often that a serviceman's face is found fault with, but it is reported that on one occasion when Admiral Sir Gilbert (Monkey) Stephenson (himself liberally covered with facial hair around the cheekbones and eyes – one explanation of his nickname) was visiting the Western Isles he met two officers whose faces apparently did not seem to fit since he commented, 'In my opinion too much consideration has been given to the care and maintenance of your complexions.'

Uniformity of turn out can be insisted upon and without much difficulty be achieved but uniformity of complexions cannot often have been the requirement. There is a case on record – albeit a century ago – that when the Captain of one of Her Majesty's ships called for his gig, he noticed that 'stroke' had a black eye. To maintain uniformity the Captain ordered the rest of the crew to black one of their eyes with burnt cork!

"'AIR CUT YOU!'"
'FULL SET'
'PERMISSION TO GROW'
JUST NOT ON
"WHAT! WITH TWEEDS!"
THE UPPER LIP... ENTIRELY UNSHAVEN
"NOT THAT WORN"
"NOT LONG NOW - SIR - SHINE JUST COMING"

# III.
# MUCKING ABOUT IN BOATS.

The exchange of signals in the Royal Navy is a subject in itself to which justice has already been done and it would be impertinence for an airman or a 'pongo' to trespass on the Senior Service's preserves to any depth but the classic of the Admiral's washer-woman must be recorded.

The Admiral, flying his flag at Malta, prided himself on his immaculate turn out, which hc achieved with the help of his personal Maltese washerwoman. During a lull on Fleet exercises he was wont to call her to his ship to collect his 'smalls' and so on to be returned in double quick time perfectly laundered. Accordingly as his Flagship was approaching Malta the signal was sent 'Send Admiral's woman at once'. Flags saw at once that a correction was necessary. It was sent 'Between Admiral and woman insert washer'.

The Fleet was carrying out high speed manoeuvres and on board one of the destroyers a Member of Parliament was watching the exercises with great keenness. A sailor came up to the bridge, saluted 'A message from the Admiral' he reported. The Captain beamed, 'Read it out loud' he said. The sailor read 'Of all the blundering idiots you take the cake. You nearly rammed the flagship'. The Captain pursed his lips, glancing sideways at the MP. 'Very well,' he snapped, 'have that message decoded at once.'

Another incident on manoeuvres after the war gave rise to this exchange of signals. A destroyer, HMS Diamond, collided with HMS Swiftsure, a cruiser, whose Captain promptly made the signal 'And what do you intend to do now?' To which came the sad reply 'Buy a farm!'

During the war it was found that the American destroyers in service with the Royal Navy, being long and thin, rolled very badly in high seas. On one occasion the captain of one destroyer signalled his fellow captain 'I can see down your funnel'. To which came what might be termed the tart reply 'If you touch my stern I shall scream'.

The passage of convoys was always a hazardous business but it took more than enemy action and heavy seas to damp a British sense of humour. On one occasion after the convoy had been badly mauled by a wolf-pack of U-boats an escorting destroyer signalled the Commodore, 'Gracie Fields is making water and sinking fast'. It need scarcely be explained that the Gracie Fields was a trawler.

This signal might be an excuse to return to dry land for a moment and quote a maxim attributed – probably apocryphally – to the Duke of Wellington 'A wise man makes water when he can – a fool when he must'. At which point Clanger rings a change with 'A stitch in time saves nine but a zip saves time if you are one over the eight'. A naval officer, who had hitched a lift in an RAF aircraft found himself in that situation and asked one of the crew where the 'heads' were. In the Navy, of course, the 'loo' is known as the 'heads'. The crew member smiled indulgently and with his thumb he indicated the rear of the plane saying 'In the Royal Air Force sir, the heads are tails'.

A certain pilot had a friend who had been selected to assist in tests of the new 'Seafire' – the Royal Naval Air Arm's equivalent of the famous 'Spitfire', and he went down to a 'drome near Southampton to visit him. He begged a flight and this was granted. He took the 'Seafire' off the 'deck' to disappear like a bat out of hell over Southampton way to God knows where. He appeared again a little later and made a horribly bumpy and very fast landing. He climbed out of the new aircraft shook, as they used to say, rigid. He turned to the RN's equivalent of a 'ground crew' airman – a naval rating – and said 'I'd get your 'instrument-bashers' to take a look at that

Air Speed Indicator in there – it's all to cock'. The Able-bodied Seaman said with a quiet smile, 'Knots to you, sir'.*

Percy Prune was not the only airman who distinguished himself by being able to explain away his prangings of aircraft with an almost immediate, glib excuse. There was, for instance, a certain Sub-Lieutenant of the Fleet Air Arm who 'landed' his seaplane several fathoms above the surface of the sea. He damaged not only the plane but also himself and, from a hospital bed, explained off-handedly that he'd been flying for five hours and by the time he landed again the tide had gone out.

A certain RAF pilot, on the other hand, must have hoped that sea-level would rise a few fathoms. He was from a coastal airfield and had received orders to fly at five hundred feet over the Navy. But he got it wrong at briefing and later, when airborne, got the feeling that he was flying rather high. He was at five *thousand* feet, and he signalled to say that he felt his altitude was excessive and should he come down a bit nearer the ships? With no hesitation at all the Navy came back with instant approval of this suggestion 'since' it was added, 'we anticipate some difficulty coming up nearer to you'.

It is merely a matter of keeping station! On a training exercise during World War II a First World War submarine was pressed into service together with a similar vintage commander. At sea she was easily overhauled by a smart new destroyer commanded by a smart new officer in command. After a proper exchange of signals the captain of the sleek new craft signalled that he was making 26 knots, about 18 more than the old lady of 1918, and ended by saying 'Would you care to accompany us?' The veteran submariner replied mildly, 'No thank you – you come with us – we are about to submerge.'

'Water,' laments Lt Cmdr Bylge-Cox. 'Water, water everywhere and not a drop of the gin and the pink.'

An exercise to test 'emergency drills' was in progress

---

*Later all ASIs registered in knots not miles per hour.

on an American aircraft carrier. The officer in charge, in order to simulate damage conditions as best he could, took a great lump of chalk and drew irregular shapes on the deck and marked these 'Bomb damage, deck gone'. A late-comer to the exercise encountered one of these 'bomb holes' which prevented him from proceeding as he wanted. He made an inspired move. Taking up a lump of the officer's chalk he drew two parallel lines across the 'hole' and, after writing between them 'NINE INCH PLANK', he went back to his starting point, ran across the 'plank' and joined the others.

Jack didn't approve of women sailors but when he saw a pretty little WREN carrying a heavy suitcase and dragging a kit bag along the platform at Paddington Station to her train he felt it was all wrong. He went over to her ''Ere, duck' he said, 'let me 'elp you.' Flushed, the girl breathed her thanks. The brawny stoker took her kit bag by the cord fastening the top and, suspending it from his right hand, gave it an expert kick so that it swung onto his right shoulder with ease. 'That's 'ow it's done luvvy' said the gallant. He then transferred the kit-bag to the WREN's right shoulder, hitched up his pants and made off towards the bar.

This story is told of the late Air Marshal Sir Robert Saundby, who was wartime second in command to 'Bomber' Harris. At one time at the Air Ministry he was dealing with some lengthy and turgid communications from the Admiralty in which 'their Lordships disapproved of this, their Lordships viewed that with disfavour, their Lordships felt that...' and so on. The distinguished airman, having had his fill of their Lordships replied briefly that he would bring their communications to the notice of their 'Airships'.

"HAVE THAT MESSAGE DECODED AT ONCE"
"KNOTS TO YOU~ SIR"
"....SIR, THE HEADS ARE TAILS"
"WE ANTICIPATE ... DIFFICULTY COMING UP ..."
THE TIDE HAD GONE OUT

# IV.
# FUN AND GAMES.

The serviceman in search of fun likes to 'get off the camp' and best of all to indulge in a spot of 'leaf', of which he will scrounge as much as possible, thereby following eighteenth century advice to officers to apply for leave at all times and places so that it came to be accepted that they were entitled. Leave by tradition has always been a 'privilege' although the only privilege about it was being allowed to apply at all. The applicant seldom got his fair whack. But there have always been ways of obtaining a little extra. Compassionate leave is one. An enterprising young officer applied for compassionate leave on the grounds that his wife was going to have a baby. Leave was granted. On his return he was naturally asked in the Mess whether it was a girl or a boy. He replied nonchalantly, 'Oh, we won't know for nine months or so'.

Even more saucy was the airman who presented himself before his squadron Warrant Officer for a leave pass to be signed – best blue freshly pressed, his boots gleaming and his brasses shining. Why, asked the WO did he want leave?

The erk grinned and said brightly 'Well sir, my fiance's goin' on her honeymoon and I'd rather like to go with her'. He did.

Another airman approached the subject more seriously and applied to go on leave to get married. The Adjutant, concerned for all ranks on the squadron, attempted some avuncular advice.

'You *are* sure about this Smith? I mean marriage is a big step, even in peacetime; will your allotment keep a wife and perhaps later a *family* going?

'Oh I'm sure, sir, after all she's working – earning more 'n I get as a matter of fact.'

'Yes, but I did mention a family Smith.'

'Not going to have any kids till the war's over, sir.'

'Oh come, Smith, you can't go against nature – it's expecting too much of you both.'

'Don't know about that, sir,' countered the erk, blushing ever so slightly, 'We've been doing all right so far.'

'Leave granted.'

In the services a cheap form of fun are the organised games and they are usually played in a spirit of fun though perhaps not always. The definition of an Army Sportsman given in the handbook of the Army Sports Control Board, and in essence common to all three services, is a model to which any sportsman in other walks of life might aspire. It is therefore surprising to meet such exchanges as these on the playing field or in the changing room.

Voice from the depths of a scrum in an inter-services rugger match.

'I say, steady on there, we came here to play, gentlemen.'

'Too true – but we didn't!'

Which services? No names, no pack drill!

Or again, in the changing room after an Army cup hockey match; an anonymous member of the winning team to his pal:

'Phew, that was a close call. I thought when that feller got into the circle he was bound to score a goal.'

His pal, 'So did I, until I caught his shirt.'

The ASCB definition exhorts the army sportsman to be modest in victory but Welshmen have their own interpretation of the word – win or lose. Listen to one in the changing room:

'I thought you played brilliantly Dai – (pause) – how did I play?

A certain AC2 had his own view of an officer's playing ability. Scratch games of football, cricket and rugby had, perforce, to be thoroughly democratic affairs, if full teams were to turn out; everybody or anybody who could be enlisted to play turned out. One winter afternoon a rugby match between two RAF squadrons was in progress and at one point a wing-commander went through for a try. He was going round to ground under the posts, when he tripped and disaster!

'You bloody idiot!' cried the AC2 in the lilting accents of the Rhonda. 'You twit! – you've dropped the bloody ball, sir.'

It was the Station Sports' Officer who arranged sport and games for members of HQ Staff and squadrons, wherever and whenever possible. The great Len Harvey was Sports' Officer at a famous Battle of Britain aerodrome but it was not he who was 'rabbiting' on to the CO of a fighter squadron about the extreme difficulties involved in getting together a rugby team to play some locals, with all the activity of war going on at the time.

He did go on a bit and the battle-worn young CO finally crossed his bows with, 'Ah yes, things are very grim. D'you know, at my last station, we actually had to cancel a cricket match just because our star batsman had a leg shot off and both the wicket keeper and our best left arm bowler were shot down over the Channel – bloody inconsiderate.'

A mini-Olympics had been organised among NATO troops and when the ground and equipment was being inspected by officers of the various nations competing an Italian colonel objected to the run-up for the high jump being of sand. It should, he insisted rather too heatedly, be of the same consistency as the track and he continued to argue and beat the air about this, though nobody else objected. A British colonel who sported the Africa Star tried to smooth (?) things over by remarking amiably, 'Oh come, Colonel, I seem to remember your chaps ran pretty well on sand in the desert.'

"....WON'T KNOW FOR NINE MONTHS OR SO"
"YOU TWIT! YOU'VE DROPPED THE BLOODY BALL ...."
"....WERE SHOT DOWN...BLOODY INCONSIDERATE"
TAKE HEED THIS FLY IS GROUNDED FOR LOW FLYING
"MY FIANCE'S GOING ON HONEYMOON AND..."
"WE'VE BEEN DOING ALRIGHT SO FAR"

# V.
# VIPS AT PLAY

Stephen Potter in his excellent 'gamesman' and 'one-upmanship' series never got around to Kingmanship. If he had, he would surely have given as an essential qualification the ability to carry off a situation that might become embarrassing. A certain RAF officer who found himself in a somewhat embarrassing situation can vouch for the veracity of this tale.

A fighter type had spent a delicious, if exhausting, 'forty-eight' with his popsie, who had a nice big house in Datchet Lane, a secondary road, hardly more than a wide lane, which left the old Bath Road opposite a pub called William the Fourth, and went through Datchet village and over the Thames to the Home Park and Windsor Castle.

It was hardly light when the leave weary pilot crawled out of a warm bed to make an early start back to his 'drome on the South East coast. He eventually emerged looking as clapped out as his old saloon car which stood in his lady friend's drive. He managed to start the jallopy and get it out of the gate, but as he attempted to turn left to take the London road his engine stalled. His battery was low and he had to start the car with the starting handle. His car was slewed across the road; his cap was on the back of his head, his eyes were bloodshot and he had the father and mother of all hangovers. He swung the handle and then jumped nervously as the well-mannered tones of an expensive car's horn sounded from the back of his. It obviously wanted to go the same way. His engine had nearly caught when that horn sounded again – more persistently. The pilot murmured an injunction to the impatient one to go and do something anatomically impossible. Again the horn was blown, as he swung again, and at this point he did respond. Without taking his hand or eyes off the starting handle, which, worn, was inclined to slip out, he leaned to his left and, with his left index and long finger gave the reverse of the 'V' sign. He swung again – his engine roared into life. The whole car shook as he scrambled into the driving seat – desperate to keep her going. He drove to the grass verge and waved on the driver behind – again with two rigid fingers. A large staff car went past, flying an impressive pennant, an angry red-faced driver at the wheel and an equally angry Army officer beside him and, in the back the principle occupant in the uniform of a field marshal – His Majesty the King of England, laughing, as the pilot said afterwards, 'like a ruddy drain':

Whilst Royalty can, as we have seen, weather with equanimity an embarrassing moment without themselves being embarrassed they quite rightly do not appreciate rudeness or impertinence. This story illustrates how an impertinent person can be put firmly but politely in her place by a *Very* Important Person.

Queen Victoria was his great-aunt and he was the King of England's uncle. At what was then an over-ripe age for a flight lieutenant he had chosen to do a job of work at HQ Fighter Command at Bentley Priory in that lowly rank. At that HQ flight-lieutenant *was* lowly because the place was lousy with youthful wing-commanders, group-captains and with air-commodores, who were only a little older. It was disconcerting for these brass hats when they first encountered the Marquis because over his left breast pocket the flight-lieutenant had a four decker 'fruit salad' more fitting to an air-marshal.

Of course, we all agreed that he'd been 'born with most of 'em' but above and around 'Pip Squeak and Wilfred' of the First War he wore an orchidaceous display of great orders, British and foreign, and someone in the Mess once remarked that had he qualified as a pilot and had wings, they'd have been on his back.

On the occasion of the departure of the Commander in Chief for a posting abroad a party was arranged and whilst the Marquis and some others were enjoying a drink at the bar an awful woman approached. She was the wife of an air-commodore who had recently been posted to HQ but she had already made a name for herself as a snob, who wouldn't speak to anybody below her husband's rank – unless they offered her a large gin when she might have said 'Thank you'. Her husband had been in the RAF for donkey's years and wore a modest set of medal ribbons but nothing approaching the 'Brock's firework display' of the flight-lieutenant. The lady knew her ribbons and rudely pointed to one among those worn by the Marquis. 'I say,' she said rather loudly, 'you've got the Victorian Order.' In the hush which was felt by all around her the flight-lieutenant looked down his nose at the ribbon as if noticing it for the first time then smiled cosily at the rude lady and said quietly, 'Yes, ma'am, my auntie gave it to me'.

Within the 'Airworks' there are many stories, some possibly apocryphal, about a certain titled group captain. Perhaps the favourite among airmen who served in the desert campaign – one against the 'brown jobs', the Army as a whole – is that of his entering the famous Shepheards Hotel, Cairo, and ordering three cold beers. He was with two other RAF officers and all three showed signs of weariness as they settled down to their drinks. They were in khaki desert rig, which with the addition of loosely-tied neckerchiefs, constituted the accepted uniform of desert flying types. It was not acceptable, however, to an Army officer, who, with others, was wearing exceptionally smart uniform. It was cut from gaberdine instead of the normal khaki 'drill' and earned for its wearers, usually highly placed admin officers of GHQ, the army nickname of the 'Gaberdine swine'.

After viewing the scruffy trio of bird-men with some distaste for a while, the army officer, a major, rose and approached them. 'I am Major the Honourable ..... Assistant Provost Marshal. You chaps are improperly dressed and I must ask you to leave.' The 'Groupie' looked up tiredly at the smartly attired gentleman then rose slowly to his feet, looked the officer hard in the eye and, indicating the four rank ribbons of a group-captain on his shoulder, a rank equivalent to an army colonel, replied 'And I am Group Captain the Earl of Bandon. I therefore outrank you on both counts; now kindly ..... off, there's a good chap.'

The Atcherley brothers, David (Batchy) and Dick were

legendary figures in the Royal Air Force with much service in against a background of the pre-war Schneider Trophy air races. They were nearly as well-known to the general public as to the RAF for their irrepressible antics in the air. Dick scored off the equally irrepressible Earl of Bandon in post-war days when the 'sound barrier' was much in the news whilst jets replaced the 'prop' jobs. The Earl, as an Air Marshal, landed on a Number 12 Group aerodrome in a Vampire and then went clean through the perimeter hedge. Air Officer Commanding 12 Group, Air Marshal Dick Atcherley, sent his congratulatory signal to the Earl from HQ 'on being the first officer of Air Rank to go through the barrier', adding 'We heard the bang from here'.

Here is an RAF classic oft-repeated. A hoary veteran of the Royal Flying Corps, an air commodore, was flying as a passenger in a seaplane to visit friends at a South Coast station which was equipped on one side of the hangars with a grass runway for wheeled aircraft and on the other with slipways for the reception of the kind of seaplane the air commodore was in.

As the station was approached the old boy asked the pilot whether he might make the landing. The pilot was in no position to refuse the request from such a distinguished veteran and acquiesced but when the air commodore appeared to be lining up the craft for a landing on the *grass* side, he was moved to remind him that he had floats – not wheels. The artful old chap overshot the grass runway saying something to the effect that he was 'only testing' the pilot, and, circling, made a very reasonable landing on the water and taxied toward the slipways. When the aircraft was at rest, he thanked the pilot and stepped out into three fathoms of water.

"YES, MA'AM, MY AUNTIE GAVE IT TO ME"
THE ACCEPTED UNIFORM
"LAUGHING LIKE A RUDDY DRAIN"
FFI
THANKED THE PILOT AND STEPPED OUT

# VI.
# LORDS OF THE AIR.

Let us rescue the Air Commodore from the 'drink' and return him to dry land and the days when he won his spurs as 'jockey' of a Sopwith Scout. During that period of the First War when the Army was so inextricably mixed up with the RFC that pilots were ordered not to tether their horses too near the aircraft, a Royal Flying Corps pilot landed on an airfield, which was not his own, because he believed that his engine was on the blink. He was greeted by the very doyen of all sergeant-majors of the really old school – pre-1914 vintage – and he said to him that he believed one of his cylinders was missing. He then walked off towards what he hoped was a mess tent for beer. The sergeant-major, no aircraft technician, at least knew what a cylinder was. He walked stiffly round the 'plane pace stick tucked under his left arm counting, 'One, two, three, four, five, six, seven'. Then he followed the pilot, catching him up as he was about to go through the tent flap, flung him up a perfect salute and bawled, 'Cylinders all present and correct, SAH!'

The Royal Flying Corps was a band of brothers in those days. One of them, a veteran of the First War but now too old to fly, was doing his stint in the Second as Adjutant of a station. His faded wings surmounted all the right 'gongs' over his left breast pocket. He was affectionately known to the pilots as 'Auntie' for he was a most patient and understanding gentleman but he did get a little tired of a certain 'sprog' pilot, who pestered him with interminable questions about 'the *old* Royal Flying Corps'.

'What was your *number*, Auntie?' the young one asked. 'Auntie' smiled and with no heat at all replied: 'My boy, *we* didn't have numbers, we all knew each other.'

There have been changes since his day; in more recent post-war years, when Silver Cities Airways took passengers to Le Touquet from Lydd airport, a rather nervous-seeming tripper turned to a 'handle-bar' moustached character sitting beside him as they trundled out for the take-off and said tentatively, 'Rather old aircraft, isn't it?' He was obviously a 'first timer'. 'Oh, I dunno,' said the veteran ex-flyer breezily, 'those I flew first had outside sanitation.'

As all flyers and most other people know, an aircraft should take off and land into the wind – hence those odd-looking windsocks which fly from a mast at the edge of 'dromes. An RAF instructor took a pupil up for a last run over of take-off and landing procedures. He landed the aircraft himself and then told the trainee to taxi out, take off and climb to 2000 feet. He was put out somewhat by the pupil asking, 'Shall I take off into the wind, sir, or in the direction you have just landed?'

Some things are better left unsaid. It is believed that it might have been PO Prune who, when asked during his flying training whether he had flown solo enquired, 'How low is *so* low?' But on the runway with no wheels is too low. A huge aircraft was only mid way on its lumbering take off on one of its seemingly interminable missions when the captain of the aircraft noticed that his second pilot was looking very cast down. Feeling that he should set an example as 'Skipper' he grinned and yelled 'CHEER UP!' He was then bug-eyed to see his second-in-command come out of his glum brown study to move the undercarriage lever to 'landing *gear up*'.

The Flying Officer had so many hours 'in' that he should have known better but Homer himself is said to have nodded. The FO landed with his brakes on and in that fashion which Prune always described as a "perfect three-point landing – one prop and two wheels". He got out unhurt, emerged from the dust cloud he'd caused, and said to a wing commander who was running towards the prang, 'Something must have tripped me up.'

The aircrew of a bomber had as fortunate an escape. The great bomber was severely shot up and made a very ragged landing. She slewed and bumped across the field to come to a halt near the boundary of the 'drome and the crew piled out just before she went up in flames. The next day she was a sad, blackened wreck but one of the crew had fixed a notice on a spar – it amounted to a prayer of thanksgiving; they had so nearly 'had their chips' – under the time and date of their escape was written '*WE*'RE NOT FRYING TONIGHT'.

Birds of a feather, it is said, flock together; but they should still be beware of the company they keep. There was a very brief exchange between the pilot of a twin-jet aircraft and Control when, immediately after take-off, the pilot reported that 'he'd flamed one engine out' adding that he'd flown into a flock of seagulls over the field and one had whipped through one of his intakes. 'Which one?' asked the Controller. 'Now how the hell should I know' said the pilot patiently. 'To me one bloody seagull's the same as any other.'

In 'The Passing of P.O. Prune'* the author instances the case of a Gallic Prune who gave him the inspiration for the French character 'Aspirant Praline'. Maurice, a pilot serving in the Free French Air Force, was described by his embarrassed compatriots as 'unfortunate' – so unfortunate, having destroyed several allied aircraft, that (as Prune was later) he was said to be recommended for the Iron Cross.

At the party held at the Hyde Park Hotel by the CO, the renowned René Mouchotte, to celebrate the thousandth enemy aircraft shot down by pilots flying out of Biggin Hill, Maurice was asked 'how he was getting on?' Maurice a shortish, roly-poly sort of chap, admitted shyly that he had 'got a 'Un' that day – a triumph for Maurice! His inquisitor could not get him to talk about it but in conversation with the great Rene he said wasn't it marvellous about Maurice? 'What did 'e tell you' asked the CO. 'Well he didn't actually *say* so, but didn't he shoot down an enemy aircraft?' Commandant Mouchotte, who had shared the thousandth aircraft with Squadron Leader M Charles, a brilliant Canadian pilot, shook his head and

---

* *The Passing of P.O. Prune by Bill Hooper; Midas Books.*

said rather sadly, 'No, Maurice collided with 'im over the Channel'. For Maurice this was a victory and it suggests that while he was a French 'Prune' the German pilot with whom he collided must have been some Teutonic type of the same sort.

An imitator of Maurice stood before *his* Commanding Officer in the embarrassing presence of two British Officers at an enquiry into loss of the plane with which *he* had collided (the British pilot had fortunately escaped) and the considerable damage to his own Spitfire. English was spoken. 'How,' asked the British Group Captain at one point, 'do you think this accident could have been avoided?' The immaculate young Frenchman smiled pleasantly, though a little sadly, 'I think sir, these crashes would not 'appen if I did not flew on that day.'

Collisions may have been restricted to Prunes and Pralines but crashes were not unknown. A certain squadron – one of those under the command of a high ranking officer in the RAF, a great leader of men – earned for itself a bad record for unnecessary ploughings in on landings and take-offs. He visited the station and gave the pilots some very straight talk and finished with advice to those in command regarding *their* 'finger' trouble. He wound up 'Mark you, gentlemen, those are only my suggestions but,' here he turned a very hard look toward the chastened-looking Squadron Leader and his Flight Leaders, 'just bear in mind who made 'em.'

Prune puts his finger in the pie to make the profound pronouncement, 'Many prangs make *night* work (– in the repair shops).'

He was a temporarily 'caged bird', a very young officer attached for a while to the staff of the Commander in Chief at a Command HQ. After a fortnight there he'd had only a brief meeting with the CinC and only occasionally seen him from afar. One morning they encountered each other in a narrow corridor and got into one of those silly involuntary 'dances' with one stepping out of the other's path and that one going the same way. After three of these abortive side-steppings, when the C in C stepped to starboard and the junior went to his port and they still faced each other, the great man smiled in avuncular fashion at the furiously blushing pilot officer and said, 'Would you mind very much if we sat the next one out.'

Some folk may have wondered why the RAF called propellers just that and did not continue using the more sophisticated term – airscrew. The change was made after a request for two dozen airscrews for a certain type of light bomber was sent to the Air Ministry and a matter of days later twenty-four fully trained men turned up.

Three groundcrew replacements for a bomber station did turn out as required to be as bods, not props and while the oddity of their names may have been pure blind chance, it could as easily have been the result of some quirk of humour from the person responsible for their posting. They arrived very late at the Guard Room and their breath smelt of the beers they'd had on their way from the railway station to the camp. The sergeant in charge could smell it from where he sat.

'What's your name?' he asked the first erk.

'Potts, sergeant' replied the airman.

'And what's *your* name?' he enquired of the second in the short row.

'Philpott, sarnt.'

The sergeant looked under his brows at the trio and then addressed the third, a very tall thin airman, 'And I suppose *your* name is Pisspott?' he suggested. The erk grinned and said helpfully in a high-pitched voice, 'No sergeant – but it *is* Chambers.'

What's in a name? or a nickname for that matter. Georgie was a playful pest but he was, nevertheless, sorely missed when he was shot down in the battles of 1940. To give a sample of his brand of humour, he once took a sheet of grease-proof paper, smeared it all over with mustard pickle juice and then put it in the yellowy varnished seat of the Station Commander's chair at the Mess table. It was after the CO was seen to walk away from table wearing the sheet of yellow paper on the seat of his pants that another spark gave him a nickname which, like the pickle paper, stuck for quite a while.

That the CO was not unaware of what went on in his command was evident a matter of forty-eight hours later when Georgie, from 'B' Flight hut, attempted to contact a buddy of his, then in the Intelligence Room, on the 'phone. Georgie got through to what he believed to be the required extension and prattled on about going into Town 'for a thrash' that night. On being told the rendezvous the voice which had answered the 'phone asked 'Where's that?' Now Georgie and his pal practically lived in that club when on leave so Georgie quite naturally said, 'I say, that *is* you isn't it Ginger?'

'No this, Pilot Officer ...., is old Mutton-Arse.'

Modern communication equipment is sometimes treacherous! A bomber was returning from a particularly hazardour 'op' and the pilot was tired and irritable enough to say, when the WAAF who acknowledged his request to land immediately asked him to orbit the field, 'Silly little cow'. He'd forgotten to take his finger off the 'transmit' button but did so when he saw it was at 'transmit' – but not before he heard the WAAF's acknowledgement 'Mooooo'.

COLLIDED WITH HIM OVER THE CHANNEL."
"ALL PRESENT AND CORRECT SAH!"
"....WE ALL KNEW EACH OTHER"
"...WOULD NOT 'APPEN IF I DID NOT FLEW..."
"...HAD OUTSIDE SANITATION!"
"SOMETHING MUST HAVE TRIPPED ME"

# VII. BRAND'S ESSENCE.

It is but a step from a cow to an ox and thence to Oxo, Bovril and such-like concentrates as Brand's Essence, a popular food for invalids in pre-war days. An essence of quite a different kind but one which might well waken the dead used to emerge from the mouth of RSM 'Bosom' Brand and his accomplices, the CSMs, at Sandhurst. Guards drill sergeants and sergeant-majors – RSM Brand's accomplices at the RMC all came from the Guards – are remarkable for their incredible command and use of the English language. Their scathing comments, always colourful, sometimes erudite, were always entertaining – except to the recipient of their vocal barrage. Some typical doses of RSM Brand's essence follow.

The CSMs – and much more so the RSM – enjoyed immunity from the laws of lesé majesté. In fact, if the pun is permissible, lazy majesty did not escape the lash of the King of the Square's tongue, as King Hussein of Jordan discovered when RSM Brand addressed him in these words: 'Mr King Hussein, sir, you're the most idle King Cadet it has been my misfortune to try to drill sir.'

On marching and foot drill he had this to say 'We don't stamp our feet, we DRIVE THEM INTO THE GROUND'. With modern rubber soled boots this reamrk has lost much of its point but the remark of a CSM commenting on the efforts of Mr Lutine-Bell to master the art of slow-marching lost none. 'Mr Loootine-Bell sir, you're walking round the square like some strange bird, sir.'

After having passed many hundreds, if not thousands of cadets off the square 'Bosom' could still not quite fathom them. The depths of despair can be detected in his cry: 'You young gentlemen don't behave like young gentlemen; you behave like foolish persons.' Of course, this cry was wrung from him by OCTU* cadets – not his familiar pre-war gentlemen cadets, who naturally always behaved like young gentlemen. Or did they always?

Sometimes a hapless cadet got a measure of his own back but never from 'Bosom'. Once a staff sergeant riding instructor (this is going back a bit) got a smart return of service when to his sarcastic comment 'Mr Prince Abdullah, sir, you should be riding a camel', he received the ace, 'I have Staff, since I was a little boy.'

The late King Farouk of Egypt was a Gentleman (wily oriental type) Cadet at the Shop (the RMA* Woolwich). He therefore escaped being dosed with Brand's essence – more's the pity – it should have done him good. He left at the end of his first term to ascend the throne on the death of his father. The treatment he received as a 'Snooker' (first termer) at the Shop is supposed to have been the root cause of his hatred of the British. If he had stayed long enough to become a senior how he would have delighted in tormenting snookers and how different his future might have been. As it was he did not love the British and the British soldier wasted no love on him either.

The story of an Army driver, whose truck collided with the staff car in which King Farouk was travelling went the desert rounds. On an early run from one base to another, rounding a bend, he had a near-miss (after all a near-miss is strictly speaking a hit, or so the RAF have it) with the big car. No great damage was sustained by either vehicle and there were no injuries but the army driver was informed that the principal of the three people in the staff car was His Majesty, King Farouk.

Back at his base the driver set about making his report and wrote something to this effect: 'Proceeding along the road from Tel el Kebir to Abbasia at 0800 hrs ..... I collided with a staff car number ..... containing three wogs .....' His sergeant, who may not have been aware that the British policy at the time was to court the good offices of the king, was, nevertheless, aghast. After

*Officer Cadet Training Unit

*Royal Military Academy

calling the driver some appropriate names he said that the CO would 'do his nut' if *that* report went through and he told the driver to rewrite. The private did 'Proceeding along the road ..... etc etc ..... I collided with a staff car containing His Majesty King Farouk and two other wogs.'

"DRIVE THEM INTO THE GROUND!"
"COLLIDED WITH A STAFF CAR... CONTAINING THREE WOGS"
"I HAVE ... SINCE I WAS A LITTLE BOY!"
"... THOUSANDS OF CADETS 'OFF THE SQUARE' TO GLORY...."

# VIII. ALCOHOL AND SUTURES.

Horace in one of his Odes has a couplet which might be freely translated as 'Who after a drink or two worries about rough soldiering or retired pay (poverty).' Indeed a pocket flask is a piece of a soldier's kit, but like ammunition its contents should not be expended thoughtlessly. In the 1914-18 war, claims one who served in it, being drunk meant something. On one occasion he found one of his men lying on the ground, as he thought, dead drunk. But his sergeant said ''E ain't really drunk sir, I saw 'im move 'is arm.'

The definition of drunkenness as opposed to 'drink taken', is often under dispute. In the hey-day of Vine Street police station the presiding magistrate had to deal with two officers on the morning after a particularly heavy celebration – the Regimental dinner had coincided with the promotion of one of them. He defined it – or to be more accurate failed to define it – in these words. First we have the drunks, then the drunk and disorderlies, then the drunk and incapable and then – then we have your friend Captain .....'

'Too true' beams Clanger, 'many people in the glass-house were thrown there because they were stoned.'

Teetotalism is seldom an excuse for drunkenness but it has been known to be given as one. A Flying Officer was heavily hungover and haggard as he faced his CO, on the mat, for being drunk and incapable the night before. He was apologetic, 'I do realise that I was intoxicated on my return to the station last night, sir' he said. And he went on to explain (as he felt quite reasonably) 'I went to this "charity do" with two other officers and I won a bottle of scotch in a raffle – and neither of the other two bods drink scotch.'

In the dim past at a camp at Seaford an anonymous territorial hailed his company cook, who was making preparations for night 'ops' with 'Are you taking tea or coffee in the dixies?'

'What the hell! Why do you want to know? and my name's Beer by the way.' (And it was too!) 'I am uncertain whether to put rum or whiskey in my flask.'

There was a soldier with sound administrative forethought. Napoleon it is known put water in his wine – pre-phyllexera Chambertin too – he deserved to be beaten!

In the Royal Navy, where they only put the minimum water in their Plymouth, empty bottles are sometimes referred to as 'dead Marines' for the following reason. William IV, the sailor king, when Duke of Clarence had been dining on his ship and noticed and pointed to some empty bottles 'Take away those dead marines' he said. A certain Major of Marines – one can picture him so well – took umbrage and said, 'May I respectfully ask your Royal Highness why you apply the name of the Corps, to which I have the honour to belong, to those empty bottles.' The Duke with tact and very quick wit replied, 'I call them marines because they are honest fellows who have done their duty and are now quite ready to do it again'.

This explanation seemed to mollify the proud but somewhat pompous Major. There must have been a shortage of port bottles in those days – now it is milk!

Whatever the definition of drunkenness may be the morning after is the same for all of us! Even without the aid of Bacchus the morning can find us not quite up to the mark. At a certain regimental HQ an officer was heard lamenting 'I'm not the man I was; but I *was*.' How well we know that feeling, but his lament would not receive any sympathy on sick parade. The Army approaches sick parade like any other parade – regimentally – in fact a zealous Lance-Corporal has been heard to bellow 'Double up those sick.' Presumably a man too sick to walk would have to detail a proxy to double for him!

At least King George V at the time of his severe illness had a sympathiser in a CSM of the Cameron Highlanders. When duties were being mounted on Edinburgh Castle esplanade the inspecting officer came on a particularly dirty and idle soldier, 'Take his name sergeant-major.'

As the duty Warrant Officer was doing so and writing in his little black book he addressed the offender thus; 'No wonder the poor King takes bad when he thinks he is paying two shillings a day for the likes of you.'

A poor landing by parachute can be painful but it is preferable to a 'Roman candle'. A sergeant pilot was returning from a sweep on occupied France. He was in trouble; his 'plane had been badly knocked about and the engine was failing. Over Kent he had to take to his parachute but made a very poor landing, being dragged through the tree tops, finally dropping through the branches of a big tree to land sprawling across some barbed wire. He'd been lucky, however, to get away with a broken leg, broken arm and many cuts and scratches about face and hands but in hospital, swathed in yards of bandage, he looked much worse than in fact he was. Of course he caught the attention of a kindly local lady who used to visit the hospital bringing small comforts to the patients. She approached the sergeant's bed. He'd been snoozing and lay quite still. 'You poor, poor boy,' clucked the dear lady, 'whatever happened to you?'

The sergeant was in the best of spirits and roused himself.

'Oh nothing much ma'am' he said, 'I just had a nasty fall.'

'What did you fall from?' enquired the visitor.

'About 1,300 feet lady.'

Yet another example of the reputed lack of high intellect displayed by the RAF's sergeant-major, the Station Warrant Officer, and there are many such quoted, is given in the case of an airman applying to the WO for a 12-hour pass for the following Saturday. The WO eyed this too-posh-spoken leading aircraftsman and asked why he wanted leave of absence. The airman said brightly that he 'wanted to see Dr Malcolm Sergeant'. 'I' said the WO, pointing to what was known as the 'Tate and Lyle syrup trade mark' on his cap but which is in fact the royal coat of arms, 'am a Warrant Officer First Class, airman – *not* a sergeant!' The airman tried to explain 'Oh no sir, not

Doctor Malcolm – sergeant, but Dr Malcolm Sergeant. Sergeant, sir, is his surname.' The WO was no longer interested. 'No pass; you're not pushing off to some posh civvy doctor. If the camp MO isn't good enough for you – carry on suffering.'

"THEN WE HAVE YOUR FRIEND CAPTAIN . . . ."
ESTAMI
"'E AIN'T *REALLY* DRUNK SIR~"
"I WON A BOTTLE OF SCOTCH"
"YOU POOR BOY! WHATEVER HAPPENED TO YOU?"
HE DESERVED TO BE BEATEN
SICK QU ERS
"DOUBLE UP THOSE SICK!"

# IX. GROUNDED.

Get on ..... PARADE. Punctuality is practically a fetish in the Army and not without good reason; in action to cross the starting line before zero hour is as bad as being too late. In barracks, however, a soldier is reckoned to be late unless he is at the appointed place at least five minutes before the appointed time. Our old friends Major Boyne and Captain FitzGerald were discussing the matter of punctuality, indirectly in connection with their favourite pastime. 'Tell me Major,' said Captain FitzGerald, 'do you believe in sex before marraige?' The Major gave the question his deepest consideration and at length replied, 'Well, Desmond, no; not if it's going to make you late for the service.'

Punctuality is no more than strict compliance with orders. A soldier has to be conversant with many sets of orders; Garrison orders; battalion standing orders; routine orders; orders for sentries and last but by no means least, Fire Orders. The observance of the last put a certain officer cadet, training at Shorncliffe in the bitter winter of 1939, in a quandary. The squad was doing what the sergeant called ' and and foot' in order to warm up. This consisted in 'marking time' smartly, knees well up, at the same time swinging the arms and hands up together as if clashing cymbals. This increased the bodily heat, but not so much as experienced by Officer Cadet Gore-Booth.

His vigorous efforts drew from the sergeant the cry 'Mr Gore-Booth, sir, you're on fiierr sir.' Mr Gore-Booth took no notice. He had been trapped by that sergeant before. He merely continued his 'and and foot with more vigour. Again the cry rang out 'MISTER Gore-Booth, you're on FIIÈRR SIR.' Sure enough he was. His enthusiastic 'and and foot had ignited a packet of book matches in his battle dress thigh pocket, which was now smouldering nicely. The problem facing Mr Gore-Booth was how to comply correctly with Fire Orders. These enjoined the person discovering the fire to shout FIRE and try to put it out. It seemed to Mr Gore-Booth pointless to add his feeble cry to the sergeant's stentorian 'FIIERR' so it only remained to put it out. It seemed silly to make a dash for the nearest static water tank and plunge in and as silly to roll in the snow in an endeavour to put it out. To plunge his woollen-gloved hand into his pocket and extract the matches would only run the risk of committing the heinous offence of 'spreading the conflagration'. His gloves would catch fire. But this the increasing pain in his leg forced him to do. This heroic behaviour earned him no commendation. The sergeant merely told him to double off parade before he put him on a charge of being improperly dressed.

Many a soldier asked his opinion of soldiering might say that his days were spent on spud peeling and other such fatigues and that most of his nights were spent on guard allowing, as one sentry put it, 'no unauthorised persons to loiter in the virginity of his post'. The normal exchange between a sentry and an unauthorised, or even authorised, person approaching his post is 'Halt, who goes there?' – 'Friend.' – 'Advance friend and be recognised.' This ritual has at times been varied by sentries in many ways ranging from the exchange between a sentry on the main gate guard of HMS King Alfred and the challenged person of 'Halt, who goes there?' – 'Friend.' – 'Advance friend and pay me the one and nine pence you owe me', to the challenge of the elderly Home Guard private (obviously a retired general) who, with moustache bristling above a smoking shot gun, cried 'Who went there?'

In a certain unit that shall be nameless the routine was varied by the Colonel himself challenging the sentry as he approached his post with 'What ho within!' To which the sentry instantly and commendably replied 'What ho without!'

One challenge given by a sentry on duty outside a Brigade HQ on training and overhead, to his delight, by the Brigadier in his tent, might have been more appropriate to an Israeli on guard on the Golan Heights. The sentry halted his 'victim' who however declared himself to be a 'foe'. Whereupon the sentry invited him 'to advance and be circumcised'.

As has been seen, a sentry has been suspected of asking his CO for a light for an illegal fag and Officer Cadet Gore-Booth was definitely guilty of smoking on parade. A certain member of a Home Guard unit, although a non-smoker and teetotaller, is reported to have transgressed the commandment 'Thou shalt not smoke'.

He was an insufferable snob with no conception of the term 'muck in' and was a bore to his fellow locals. He was fond of quoting all the rules and regulations and was suspected of being a 'sneak'. One evening as the unit was about to be dismissed, the 'Guardsmen' were contemplating a darts session with the CO at 'The Cricketers'. The misfit sniffed at the notion and made his way to the bus stop.

As he waited for his bus a boy came up alongside him and said, politely enough, ''Ere mister, do you know your gun's on fire?' The snooty one didn't answer this preposterous suggestion but the boy went on 'Your gun *is* alight'. He was still ignored except for a hissed 'Go away you snotty-nosed brat'. At that point his bus came along.

When he was seated he was treated to amused and surprised looks from the other passengers, which he tried to ignore. Then the bus conductor came along and said, 'Blimey, mate, you've been busy fighting 'Itler tonight; your rifle's still smoking'. The Home Guard unslung his rifle and, true enough, saw that a wisp of smoke was issuing from the barrel. Back at HQ someone behind him in the ranks had dropped a fag, which was just the right size to fit the bore, down his rifle barrel. The conductor sniffed 'Good, ain't it eh?' he said to the rest of the bus in general. 'What lengfs people will go to to 'ave a sly puff – on the lower deck too.'

In the 1914-18 war young soldiers were advised to note whether the fuse of a grenade or of an explosive charge was smoking because they were told 'they generally fizzes before they goes off'. A young private on the beaches outside Dunkirk in the last 'Lot' might have profited by this advice. He was crouching face down in a bomb crater during a straffing when something big landed on his back. 'WHA'SAT F'CRISAKE?' he yelled. 'Me' came the reply near his ear. 'Who's me?' said the private, calmer, but with his face still well down between folded arms. 'Your corporal twit', the newcomer to the hole said, 'Oh thank Gawd! For a second or two I thought you was going to explode.'

The V1 gave due warning that it was going to explode by cutting its engine. Nicholas whom we have already met is the reporter of this flying bomb contretempts. He became a paratrooper and subsequently a rather turbulent prisoner of war. Something of what we like to call 'the British sense of humour' must have brushed off his British father on to Nick in that he displayed a talent for observant humour which is, to us, unexpected in a Scandinavian.

One very cold morning, he relates, he assembled with other POWs at a roll call before being marched to the coal mines nearby to dig coal for Hitler. The Camp Commandant was a 'little Nazi bastard', according to Nicholas, and swaggering in the murk of this drab morning, he obviously had something of moment to say to the assembled British prisoners.

'Goot morning chentlemen.' No response from the ranks. 'Enklant is now kaput! The Fuhrer has announced that his secret veapon, a flyink pomb, has destroyed the South Coast of Enklant from Remsgate to South'empton.' He strutted in his jack boots before the prisoners, his staff officers exchanging reassuring smirks; still no audible or visible response from the 'rude soldiery'. Then a voice from the ranks, in the accents of the 'Ome Counties enquired, 'Did Portsmuff get done as well?'

'Yaa!' cried the Commandant triumphantly, 'Bortsmut is destroyed gombletely!' Silence – then the same voice said thankfully, 'Fank Christ for that! Never did like that ..... tahn.'

The POWs fell about laughing while the Commandant screamed for order – even drawing his Luger to menace them.

But there was one old lady in Portsmouth for whom Hitler's raid meant little. When the sirens sounded the

'Alert' she rang the bell for her maid and when she arrived instructed her 'Daisy, go and see if the cellar flap is down'.

Commanding Officers are often most anxious to learn their nickname, if, unlike 'Old Mutton-Arse', they have not got their ears to the ground and have already found out. One CO badgered his adjutant relentlessly to tell him what his command called him in private until at last the 'adj' confessed that 'Sir's' cognomen was 'Old Thrombosis'. 'Thrombosis?' queried the Colonel. 'Yes' explained the Adjutant. 'It's a medical term I believe', and escaped to his own office. The CO sent for a medical dictionary and discovered that he was 'a large clot which if disturbed is liable to upset the whole system'.

Two characters in ITMA – Tommy Handley's wartime radio show – used to raise a routine laugh by concluding their 'piece' with the exchange of courtesies – 'After you Claud', 'No after *you* Cecil'. The sergeant in this tale had the same idea but was not quite so courteous.

During a desperate drive towards the Rhine, in the closing stages of the last war, a young officer found himself with the remnants of his command under sudden, intense and concentrated fire from the enemy. All had their heads well down – most of them praying – when the young 2nd Lieutenant wanted to pass on an order to his trusted, veteran, sergeant. He called out 'Sergeant, I want you. Where are you?' During a brief lull in the explosions around; he got the acknowledgement 'I'm over to your right sir.' 'I can't locate you sergeant; stand up so that I can see you.' As soon as he had said the words he could have bitten his tongue off. He got the reply he later admitted he had deserved. 'You want to see me sir, *you* bloody stand up.'

Whitehall Warriors have always come in for more than their fair share of derision. The RAF example of the species – a 'caged bird', that is a pilot temporarily grounded to occupy a desk job was walking down Whitehall when a civilian stopped and enquired 'which side the War Office was on?' The RAF type pondered a moment, then said, 'Ours I *think*'.

"WHO WENT THERE ?"
"YOUR CORPORAL-TWIT!"
"YOUR GUN'S ON FIRE"
"OURS, I THINK."

# X.
# FINGER.

Finger trouble in the Royal Air Force is in no way related to, nor can be likened to, trench feet in the Army so a few words of explanation might not be out of place here. The Most Highly Derogatory Order of the Irremovable Finger was a most doubtful wartime Royal Air Force distinction which nobody wanted to earn – but quite a few did. It was awarded for all kinds of boobs and blacks committed not only by aircrew members, but also by ground personnel and recipients were duly 'gazetted' in the RAF's official training memorandum – a monthly publication called TEE EMM.

The Order was instituted by the Editor, Squadron Leader Anthony Armstrong Willis, OBE, MC, who in peacetime was the famous playwright of 'Ten Minute Alibi' and he was A.A. of Punch and the author of a whole parade of funny books about the regular army of the years after the first war.

Naturally PO Prune, that gallant but bird-brained pilot and doyen of all RAF clanger-droppers, became Patron of the Order. 'Finger' was the single word admonition to 'wake up', 'get cracking', or as the army have it, to 'extract a digit'. The subject is dealt with at length in the life story of Pilot Officer Percy Prune – The Passing of Pilot Officer Prune – here, in this collection of clangers and boobs we can give but a handful of instances of the special kind of RAF balls-up which could have earned the individuals concerned the award of the 'Highly Derogatory Order'.

'Finger trouble' infected the WAAF as well as the RAF. A WAAF on telephone duty received a report from the Duty Officer, as part of his job, which she, as part of her job, had to pass on, that a Spitfire, due at the station at 1050 hours, was now overdue.

'Spitfire' mused the girl, 'is that a monoplane or biplane sir?'

Patiently the 'Duty Dog' explained that not only was a Spitfire a monoplane, it was also one of the two best known single-seater fighter aircraft in the service. The WAAF thanked him for this information and then asked briskly, 'How many are there in the crew sir?'

'I had nothing on the clock but the maker's name' was regarded as the classic low-flying line-shoot, but altimeters – like a car's speedometer – must start *somewhere*. A certain Pilot Officer could not have realised this when, after taking his Mustang through some high tension cables, which carried a load of 120,000 volts, removing three insulators, 200 yards of one inch cable plus 120 yards of telephone wire, complete with pole, he landed what remained of his aircraft with commendable skill. When told by his CO that he must have been flying at less than fifty feet, he replied 'That can't be true sir, my altimeter showed 500 feet, so I must have been at that height'.

When a Pilot is about to land in a more orthodox manner, there are warning methods to show whether the undercarriage is down and locked. One was a loud klaxon horn which gave the pilot fair warning. This sounded on one occasion when a pilot, carrying a mixed bag of RAF people, was about to set down. There was very light, low cloud about but the pilot had things well in hand and was in one cloud and out of it all set to land – undercarriage down and locked. A young chaplain on his first ever flight was rather breathless and expressed himself delighted with the experience of flying. He thanked the pilot and then asked the question – 'Do you always sound your hooter when going through a cloud?'

A pilot under training was asked one or two questions about those undercarriage warnings. One put to him by his instructor was what action he would take if, when he was about to land, that loud klaxon sounded. The pupil replied 'I should open the throttle slightly to stop the horn blowing and then, when I had landed, I'd remove the fuse – that would stop it'.

When taking on petrol in a car on a rainy day it is advisable to see that no rain gets in the tank. It was not raining when a largish aircraft landed for refuelling on an aerodrome overseas. The bowser pipe-line dripped somewhat during this filling up and one of the crew, who had got some grease on his hands, held them under the pipeline and then rubbed his hands with a rag. No impression at all was made on the grease. Becoming horribly suspicious, the crew member took a closer look and discovered that they were drips of water – not petrol. The station water bowser had been in constant use for a while beforehand and the ground crew had, in a misguided effort to show willing to the visitors, got cracking; reached for the nearest nozzle and pumped some sixty or so gallons of water into the fuel tanks.

The MHDOIF can be awarded for action in an office as well as on the airfield. When drafting service messages it is very desirable to be brief, succinct and to the point but brevity can sometimes lead to disturbing ambiguity. A squadron leader on a large, long established aerodrome, was requested to make accurate returns as to the availability of sleeping accommodation on his station. His station, well-known in the RAF, had rows of little houses occupied in peacetime by married personnel. His return ran: 'All married officers' quarters, except Nos 8 and 9 are misappropriated in that they are used by single officers and WAAF other ranks and in all cases the floor space has been calculated according to the personnel occupying the quarters'.

They shot the sun as well as enemy planes and lines in the RAF. A Group Captain commanding a station up North must have had what the RAF used to call a 'red neck' when after passing a crew member in his car and spotting him putting something to his eye, he reversed and bawled out to the man, 'Who gave you permission to use a camera?' – only to find that the airman, a navigator, was practising taking shots with his sextant.

A young pilot indulged in a most fearful beat-up of his Squadron's 'A' Flight huts – barely scraping the roof. When he had landed and was being angrily told off by the flight commander, he was asked by that gentleman, 'Didn't you see me waving my cap?' 'No sir, I did not' he explained. 'You see I was flying on instruments at the time.'

A pupil pilot was on the chief instructor's mat for a poor showing during a low flying exercise. His minimum height above the ground should have been approximately 250 feet but was in fact, at times, much lower. On landing he had reported that his engine was overheated. Had he, the chief instructor asked, any idea why his engine had overheated? No more at a loss for an answer than Percy Prune, the pupil came back with 'Ah yes, sir, I hit a bird.'

Arriving at home base after a 'stooge' on a very dark night an aircraft, 'F' for Freddie, found no lights of any sort on the airfield. The captain tried repeatedly to contact airfield controller by R/T but without success. Then he 'beat up' the Control Tower with headlights on and had the recognition code, 'colours of the day', fired off. After twenty minutes somebody got their finger out – some lighting was provided and the patient 'F' for 'Freddie' landed and taxied to dispersal. The air bomber and navigator had got out but the 'Skipper' took a moment to collect his thoughts and then just before he took off his helmet and earphones he heard the flight lieutenant airfield controller first identify the field in code and then say 'Hullo 'F' for 'Freddie', hullo 'F' for 'Freddie', this is Control, your turn to land is number two.'

A Controller's lot, like the policeman's, is not always a happy one. During the Battle of Britain the cannibalisation of aircraft became a feverish and vitally important factor towards winning. Teams of airmen scoured the Home Counties for the wreckage of our aircraft brought down by Goering's people. They'd take a fuselage here, a main plane there, a tail unit from another damaged aircraft and try to bring all together to create a complete aircraft somehow. The bits and pieces, depending on the size, were hauled to a central point on lorries and trucks large and small.

The Controller in the Operations Room of a famous B of B airfield was somewhat startled one dark evening to learn that a certain 'Red Two' was approaching the 'drome and requesting landing instructions. He was, he said, very badly damaged but he knew that his direction was due South East of 'Home'. What was his height? His height, he said, was seven feet 'Sevenah feeeetah' he repeated. 'How the b..... how' responded the Controller, '*can* your height be sevenah – repeat sevenah feet?' The reply came from the blithe spirited aircraft fitter who was sitting in the cock-pit of a badly beat up Spitfire and using the R/T 'Coming in on a truck – repeat – coming in on a truckah – ovah!'

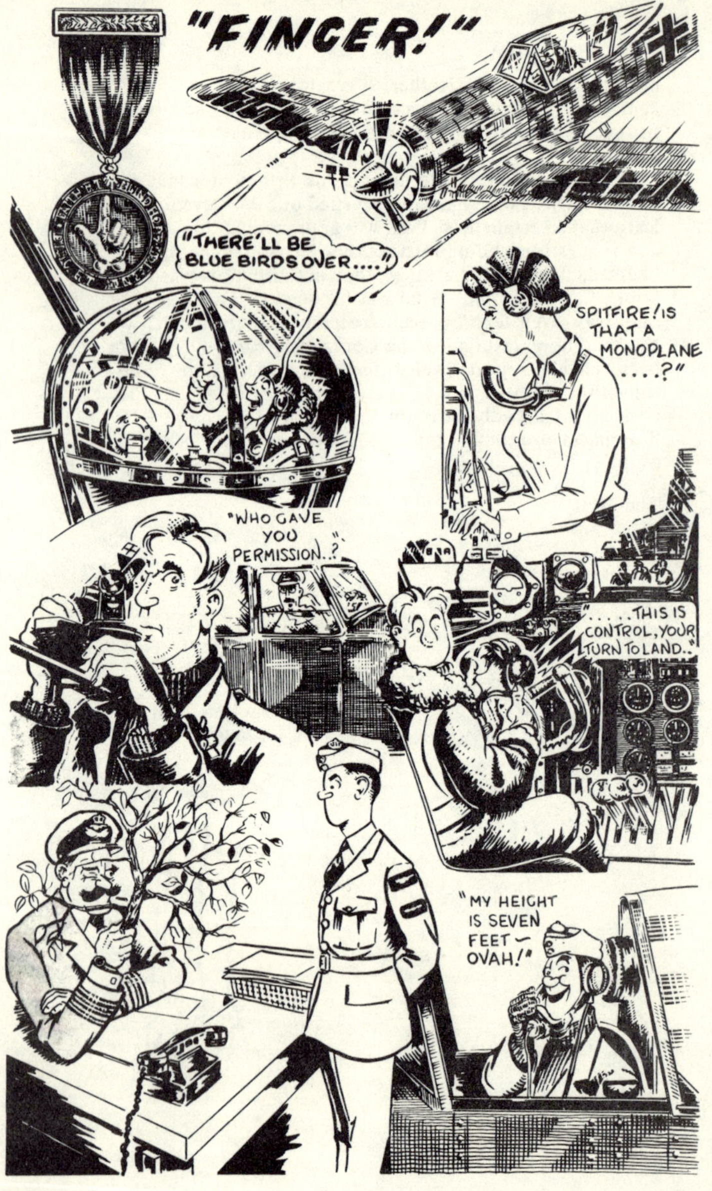
"FINGER!"
"THERE'LL BE BLUE BIRDS OVER...."
"SPITFIRE! IS THAT A MONOPLANE ....?"
"WHO GAVE YOU PERMISSION..?"
".....THIS IS CONTROL, YOUR TURN TO LAND.."
"MY HEIGHT IS SEVEN FEET — OVAH!"

# XI. FAILED B.A.

In the wartime RAF the 'drill-pig' (Corporal), his superior, the Drill-Sergeant, and *his* overlord, the Warrant Officer 'Dicip' all earned for themselves a reputation for smartness of appearance, a sound knowledge of rules and regulations but a blind ignorance of more sophisticated matters. Whether this was deserved in every case is a matter of individual opinion and personal experience but some gems based on this fixed belief among the troops are still being repeated by veterans who experienced such 'sprogs', hells as Uxbridge, Cardington and, perhaps the worst, Padgate in the early months of the war. It must be said in defence of the NCOs mentioned that they were not getting the usual peacetime recruit. They had to deal with all types who had volunteered – the sons of gentlemen farmers, young noblemen, undergraduates, medical students, ribbon salesmen, quondam milkmen, burglars, butchers and other tradesmen – you name it, they were there. While they didn't always show it, the Dicip' NCOs were a mite confused at times. Here are two well-known stories based on the fact (or fallacy) of NCO 'thickness'.

On pay parade the corporal had reported to the sergeant that all were present and that all was correct. The only character missing from the caste was the most important, the Station Warrant Officer. He came onto the parade ground, immaculate as always, after what seemed to be at least five minutes 'silence' while the troops were at attention. He marched down the ranks with his Foot-Guards' pace but was seen to halt and turn sharply to the men as a voice, in an accent which used to be called 'the Oxford accent', said wearily in the silence, 'They *also* serve who stand and wait.' The WO flushed as he eyed the ranks. 'Who said that?' he demanded. Back came the answer in a flash. 'Milton, sir, in his sonnet on blindness.'

It is said by some that the exchange went thus: ''Oo said that?' – 'Milton, sir.' – 'Alright Milton, I'll deal with you later!'

Another NCO, who was a non-flying type, whose function was the drilling and discipline of flying cadets, addressed a 'squadron' of them on the parade ground during what the RAF called a 'bad weather state' – there was very thick ground mist so that those in the rear ranks could not even see the Flight-Sergeant but heard him announce in sarcastic tones and terms which, before long he'd be in no position to address to an aircrew member, commissioned or otherwise, 'Due to a bad weather state, there won't be no flyin' for you future Lords of the Air, 'owever the H'education H'officer 'as arranged a lecture – on Keats'. He paused and then added: 'Whatever *they* are!'

The RAF even produced some authors who, hither to, did not know they 'had it in 'em'. One quiet, rather studious pilot officer had written a book. It was a very good book and well received in the Service and by the public. At a cocktail party he was approached by a rather jumped-up wing commander, who had served on the same station as the author some time before – 'Hallo there! Heard you have a book published.' 'Yes' said the PO. The wing-commander fancied himself as a wit and said 'Who wrote it for you eh?' The junior officer's own group-captain was standing nearby. He viewed the 'Wing-Co' coldly and said: 'Oh, *he* wrote it – who read it to you?'

At a school for teleprinters a WAAF officer was addressing a group of the girls who, having qualified, were about to be posted to their respective units. It was quite a pep talk finishing with 'And remember that although we are regarded as a junior service we nevertheless have considerable traditions and should set an example to other women's services and always take pride in our uniform. If at any time in the future you feel that in some way you are about to bring disgrace to that unifrom – take it off!'

A distinguished pilot, demobbed after seeing service

from the time of the Battle of Britain to the finish, returned to university to resume his studies and the battle for a BA – now just another 'civvy' with his several 'gongs' packed away with his uniform. He was late for a lecture and the don paused in his delivery to say sarcastically 'Ah! *Good*-morning – twenty minutes adrift I think you might once have called it. What would have been said to you in the RAF had you arrived late?' The ex-flyer thinking back on those many briefings before flight smiled and replied 'Oh, they'd all have stood up and said "Good morning sir!".'

In the Army in peacetime to rise to the higher ranks the soldier had to obtain his first class certificate of education. Many a first class man has failed to make CSM because he could not get his first. One of them, who simply could not pass in English when waxing eloquent at a Sergeants' Dance was heard to complain: 'I don't need to be the immortal fart of Bradford-on-Avon to be a Sarn't-Major.'

This he proved conclusively whenever he acted as CSM in the absence of the holder of the appointment, but his inability to defeat his immortal enemy deprived him of substantive promotion.

In those days it must have been assumed that the officers were illiterate because they were seldom allowed to teach. The 'professors' were regimental NCO instructors under the direction of a senior NCO or Warrant Officer of the Royal Army Education Corps. The regimental education officer himself was practically only there to organise the work and accept the rockets gracefully! He deserved sympathy as does the Indian 'schoolie' who was trying to instil the rudiments of geometry into his class. 'This' he said, drawing on the blackboard, 'is being called right angle; and this (extending the base line to make 180°) is NOT being left angle; oh no, by act of government is also being right angle.' Poor man, just as our sergeant would ever be failed first he would go through life 'failed BA'.

'Clanger' Littlewart chimes in here with 'I was quite a dab at geometry. I know that two sides of a triangle are greater than the third and that the third side of an eternal triangle is a great big square.'

One subject the officers did teach was the regimental history. An officer of the Black Watch once had an unusual class under instruction. Some members of the regiment were on a tour of the USA and the citizens of the States were much intrigued by them. Tall, gorgeously accoutred pipers in full dress, formed the background for a television interview in which the officer in charge was being asked questions about the regiment – its history and traditions. One somewhat misguided question was – 'Had the "group" ever performed in America before?' The officer, perfectly straight-faced, replied: 'Oh yes, sir, in 1776'.

Fortunately spelling is not a subject in its own right or CSM Connery of the Irish Guards would never have reached that exalted rank. At one pay parade he noticed a guardsman whom he did not recognise. 'Phwat's your name guardsman?' he asked. 'Phillips, sor.' 'Well, get up into the Fs then you ignorant idle man.'

# XII. WE DON'T NEED A MAP FOR THAT LITTLE BIT.

The hope expressed by the heading of this section echoes the RAF saying 'It will clear itself in the air' which itself conveys the same doubtful comfort as the theatrical saying 'It'll be all right on the night'.

Some of the characters in the following tales would scarcely seem, in army parlance, to have 'their feet on the ground', which is possibly an unfair state to expect of an airman!

A pilot was about to take off when he received a signal from an Aldis lamp to recall him because there was a certain mechanical defect in his aircraft about which he had not been warned. He took off just the same. When asked to account for his action – taking off against a 'white' – he was frank enough to say he'd always been used to red or green signals and didn't know what a 'white' was; but, he explained further, he had taken off assuming that the light *was* a green but that the glass had fallen out of it.

An American Army Air Force Despatching Officer certainly qualified for the 'Finger' order when briefing a crew who were to carry out a certain flight. 'If .....field is out' he said, naming a certain aerodrome, 'land. If however it is open (that is suitable for landing on) press on to .....' and he named another station.

Of course 'out' meant that the aerodrome was subject to such bad weather that it was unusable.

The first station was indeed 'out', with frost, drifting snow, ice on the runway, low cloud, strong winds and poor visibility and frequent heavy snow squalls for good measure. It was 'out' – repeat 'OUT'. Nevertheless, despite all the Controller's efforts to divert him from the evil place and to send him to an 'open' 'drome, the pilot approached and landed successfully, strictly according to the Despatching Officer's cross-fingered instructions.

Many a pilot in a jam may have wished he'd had a reverse gear. A bomb-aimer on whose identity many a veteran bomb-aimer may have pondered, must have thought his 'plane was so equipped. During his first run-in on the target he got excited and gave the captain the following instructions: 'left...left...steady, right...right... steady...left... steady, oh, blimey... back a bit...!'

That 'clearing itself in the air' bit could have been used by the flight sergeant of a certain Station Duty Flight who figures in this incident. A pilot borrowed a Moth to fly from a station near London to visit a friend on another in Devon. The 'Chiefy' of Duty Flight himself started up the aircraft and the engine was ticking over nicely when the pilot arrived to take off. He was cheerily waved away by the ground crew.

When his visit in Devon was over and he wanted to return the craft, she wouldn't start – in spite of everything every expert around tried for over an hour. Finally the pilot decided to telephone to the Station from which he borrowed the aircraft, contact the Duty Flight 'Chiefy' to ask him whether he could throw any light on the problem. He received the recipe for starting the Moth from 'Flight' who said blithely, 'Start her sir? Oh, it's quite easy when you know how; this is all you have to do. On the right side of the engine locate a piece of bakelite; now just behind that there's a chunk of metal that looks as if it's been clouted a lot with a hammer – all pitted like. Hit it hard with a hammer a few times on the dented side, then tickle the carburettor till she's flooded. Now go to the back of her and lift her tail as high as you can without banging her prop on the ground – then shake her. Have a go at starting her after that ... you'll find her all right.'

The rather dazed pilot put down the receiver after hearing what could, for him, be famous last words – 'you'll find her all right!' The recipe, however, was followed and the Moth started up without any more trouble, but the pilot did not have a moment of mental peace until he'd touched down at her home station and handed her back.

A neck that must have been decidedly puce was that of a flying instructor who, after an exercise involving beacon-flying at night with a pupil, landed very well but on the wrong 'drome. He got out of the aircraft and still unaware of his boob suggested that his pupil have a go – solo. The pupil took off and ultimately landed at the proper place – their own home 'drome. After waiting around for an hour or so the instructor discovered his boob and got a lift back by service transport.

A bomber pilot was returning from a raid in very poor visibility when he suddenly discovered that, due to an oversight he had set instruments in such a way that he'd been flying, not on the course for home, but what is known as a 'reciprocal', taking him towards the enemy. He adjusted things as best he could so that at least he was pointed for home, although at this stage he did not think he would get much further than enemy occupied Holland – if he was lucky.

His fuel gave out eventually, but he made a good forced landing in a large field and at once, according to orders, set fire to his aircraft to prevent it and its secret equipment falling into the Hun's hands. He and his crew then made off in an attempt to get to some safe place and in their turn not fall into enemy hands. They got to the edge of the flat field to find themselves outside a pub called the Rose and Crown – the 'local' of the neighbouring English village.

A certain group-captain, veteran of many, many hours flying arrived at an aerodrome in his own Moth aircraft. He was met by the Duty Pilot but was rather guarded in all his remarks about his coming to the place and the purpose of his visit. He cut enquiries short by asking his way to the Mess. On arrival there he was greeted respectfully but still remained oddly silent. Then he left the bar on what anybody would have agreed was a perfectly reasonable excuse after flight. In fact he didn't 'want one' he only wanted to take a glance at the notice board in the lobby where he could see 'Daily Routine Orders for RAF Station .....' On his return to the bar he became quite fluent and at ease – having found out at just which station he had landed!

The captain of a 'plane on a coastal patrol received some weird steering orders from his navigator; briefly these boiled down to ... a 90 degree turn left off course, then a 90 degree right turn, followed by another and then finally 90 degree turn to the left again on to the original course! The captain had remained silent throughout the three-quarters of an hour that had been spent on these manoeuvres except to acknowledge the odd directions. Now he asked 'What was *that* in aid of?' The navigator was munching a sandwich over his chart on which he had put his thermos, 'Well, Skipper, we were going towards my coffee cup and I had to get you to go round it.'

Of such navigators it was once said by an embittered pilot that if you gave a navigator more than an hour for his lunch you'd have to have him sent on a refresher course.

"WE DON'T NEED A MAP......"
"BACK A BIT – BACK A BIT!"
THE ROSE AND CROWN
LOST
RIP
HERE LIES
P.O. PRANG
"IT'LL CLEAR ITSELF IN THE AIR
F/O IVOR TWITCHE

# XIII. GOD BOTHERING.

Many a man asked why he joined the army has replied – in jest – to get a military funeral. Some may have meant it seriously because for most soldiers a military funeral would be a better send off than he would have got in 'civvy street'. Naturally like any other parade of importance a military funeral would call for a rehearsal. A certain RSM at the end of such a rehearsal concluded his instructions with this admonition to the troops, 'And as the 'earse, cortage or what-not leaves the church each man will rest on his arms reversed and will h'assume a mournful h'aspect such as any decent corpse 'as the right to expect.' Quite right too! The same RSM finally retired, became the landlord of 'The Thorns' at Horley. A small Armistice Day parade was being held at the War Memorial on the village green, where also was located The Thorns. During the two minute silence the only sound was the cawing of the rooks in the elms. Suddenly there came a most audible whisper from the landlord of The Thorns standing respectfully at his doorway 'STAND STILL THAT WOMAN'. Once a RSM always a RSM. No doubt in the private bar later he gave her a stout and a 'omily on the respect h'appropriate to the dead and h'above h'all to dead soldiers!

Not all Armistice Day services are observed on land. A wartime mob of ground-crew airmen were being transported in a veteran transport plane to another airfield 200 miles away. One aircraftsman 2nd Class had been conscripted into the RAF as a most unwilling recruit. He had never bargained for having to go into the air at all; he was strictly an earthman and now in this huge, yawing and roller-coasting, string-and-chewing-gum-constructed 'Bombay' troop carrier, he was petrified. He listened with ashen face and acute inward terror to the splutter, banging and knocking of the old aircraft's engines as he and his 'oppos' were being flown over a wide stretch of sea in turbulent weather. As he sweated there he saw an NCO aircrew member making his way along the gangway, pausing to talk to individual airmen seated each side and they immediately took off their caps looking rather solumn – as was the aircrew member. The lurid imagination of the AC2 led him to think that *this was it* – the crew member was obviously warning the troops of an imminent ditching. They had no parachutes! He couldn't have jumped if he did have one. He practically passed out when he saw a flight mate of his, whom he knew to be a devout Roman Catholic, remove his cap, cross himself and reach for the beads he always kept in his tunic pocket. This WAS it! Then the crew member came to where he squatted on his kit and bent to say, as quietly as the noise of the old aircraft would allow, 'Skipper wants to remind you that it's November the 11th, Armistice Day, and the time is now three minutes to eleven so observe the two minutes silence.'

When it came to Church Parades the Services recognised only Church of England, Roman Catholics and the all embracing Other Denominations. The first two sects provided by far the largest contingents but there were always some 'odds and sods'. A certain Warrant Officer found this out early in his long service and whenever a man claimed to be a member of some way-out sect he honoured the service practise of giving him some unpleasant job to discourage him from dodging the parade under false pretences.

On one occasion, when the various contingents had marched off, there was still one man waiting. The WO approached him grimly, 'Are you Jewish?' he asked. 'No sir,' replied the man. 'I'm a member of the Society of Friends.' 'The *what?*' The airman made it easier for the WO. 'A Quaker sir.' This was a new one on the WO but he was equal to it and he told the odd man out to go and clean the latrines. The following Sunday the WO's eagle eye spotted the Quaker lad among the C of Es and he went to stand in front of him with a vicious grin 'Got converted eh?' 'No sir,' replied the Member of the

Society of Friends. 'I'm still a Quaker but I don't like the place they have to worship in.'

The contingent from Padgate on Church Parade in Warrington contained the rawest possible sprogs in the RAF. Trying to march smartly through that dreadful snow of the first winter of the war they climbed the steps of the church and entered the portals where their dreaded bête noire, the Station Warrant Officer – who must surely have been related, if only in spirit, to the RSM of The Thorns – stood in the porch glaring balefully at each one who passed. One of them didn't get by him into the body of the church. His uniform, still smelling of long storage, his buttons not yet worn enough to take a bright polish, he went to pass the WO, looking straight ahead with his cap, dead centre, still on his head.

'AIRMAN'. Though this was hissed, to the sprogs it might just as well have been screamed and all stopped in their tracks. 'Yes, *you*' the WO continued sotto voce to the offender. 'Don't you know you can't walk into the House of the Lord with your cap on you stupid, ignorant, silly born sod.'

For all the men who may join the services in order to secure a military funeral there may be the equivalent number of women who marry into a service for a military wedding – full dress archway of swords and all that. Sometimes they can scarcely wait! There is the story – how true we wonder – of the young officer who sought out his padre for some advice just before he went on a rare forty-eight hour leave. How long, he asked the padre, would it take to get a marriage licence? In exceptional cases, the padre told him, only a matter of days. The young officer mulled this over for a moment thinking of that 'lovely weekend' in 'Room 504' planned for the near future and then asked the chaplain 'I suppose, padre, you couldn't give us a cover note over the weekend eh?'

Padres of course are often the recipients of last dying wishes and have the unhappy task of breaking the news to the bereaved. In this case they were not at the receiving end. Ginger was a well-liked airgunner. He'd joined the RAF as a boy because he was utterly alone in the world having come from a well-known 'Doctor's' orphanage. After the briefing for an extended and dangerous sortie over the North Sea he was asked by someone unaware of his lone status, in case the worst happened, who did he want notified.

The rest of the crew kept quiet. Ginger thought for a moment and then said 'Air Sea Rescue!'

Padres are sometimes called the Army 'Sky pilots', by the Royal Navy 'Holy Joes' and by all three services 'God Botherers'. A 'God botherer' was making towards the aircraft alongside the pilot – an ebullient lad. They met the CO. 'Where are you off to?' he asked. The pilot grinned, 'The padre wanted a flight sir,' he explained, 'and so we're going up to see Sir, sir, aren't we, sir?'

Perhaps they did not get so high as the pilot who is the hero of this tale. In a fighter station Mess in the closing months of the war a veteran of the '40s was being importuned by a youngster, who at this stage would probably not see much, if anything, of combat flying. 'How high had he flown in any one action?' the sprog pilot asked. The 'old' fellow, all of twenty five years, said, after a short preamble about an interception in 1940, '..... I was still climbing but at this point I didn't actually look at my altimeter but when I saw this Jerry still coming up at me from beneath I said "Oh God!", and this deep and awful voice said, "Yes my son?".'

'Coming home on a wing and a prayer', the words of that wartime sob-song, evoke the story of the advice given by a Controller in a wartime operations room to a pilot in distress. It is told in a dozen different ways. One version is that the poor chap contacted 'Ops' to report practically everything wrong with his aircraft after a sortie; almost his entire tail unit had been shot away; part of his port mainplane was gone; his engine was on the blink; his undercarriage system was damaged and while still miles from his home 'drome, he had about a pint of fuel left. To his plaintive 'what should he do?' the Controller responded solemnly 'Repeat after me ..... Our Father, which art in Heaven .....'.

"HOME ON A WING AND A PRAYER"
"REPEAT AFTER ME ~ OUR FATHER, WHICH ART IN....
"..WE'RE GOING UP TO SEE SIR-SIR!"
"....IDLE, SILLY BORN SOD!"
"...A COVER NOTE-PADRE?"
QUAKER!

# XIV. WHITE FLAG.

The motto of that renowned Irish Regiment, Slattery's Mounted Foot was 'better a coward for one day than a dead man all your life'. The order, so often given to and obeyed by the British soldier to hold a position to the last man and the last round was absolutely unheard of. Sometimes, however, honourable surrender cannot be avoided as at Calais in the last war, but surrender of any sort does not enter into even the pipe dreams of the honourable (sic) sons of the Rising Sun. It, therefore, came as a distinct surprise, when, in Burma, a Japenese officer, who turned out to be a colonel, advanced under a white flag and made it clear he wished to surrender – not a Brigade, mark you, just himself. The British, naturally, were suspicious and treated him with caution.

'You wish to surrender?' The Japanese hissed and bowed in affirmation.

'But Japanese soldiers never surrender no?'

'Iss true. Yess. Japanese *soldier* never surrenders but I am non-combatant. I am in the artirrery.'

The business of surrender is not so easy as it may sound. In the 1914-18 war a Guards CO refused to obey an order to surrender his battalion on the grounds that 'the regiment had never practised the manoeuvre in peace so could not carry it out in war'. Apart from a little 'mick-taking' the reply exemplified the Guards approach – he must have been a Grenadier – nothing but perfection is acceptable; practice makes perfect; no practice in peace, no perfection – no performance!

Sometimes a soldier may find it not too easy to surrender when he wants to, as a German soldier found in

1943 in Italy in the mountains around Radicosa. He was cold, lost and had had enough. With his hands raised he approached a foxhole occupied by some men of the US Special Service Force (The Devil's Brigade). In broken English he said 'Let me in. I want to give up. I'm lost'. He got the unexpected reply in brusque American – 'Aw – get the hell out of here, Kraut, this f.....g foxhole's full up.'

Like the Guards Officer of World War I the American Commander of the garrison of Bastogne in World War II did not know the procedure for surrendering; nor was he well versed in the diplomatic corps type language he supposed he would have to use. 'Sir, in reply to your esteemed request I have the honour to state that I regret.....' So he gave a simply phrased but highly deflationary and succinct reply 'Aw nuts!'

Not often is an ordinary and lowly civilian called upon to accept the surrender of an enemy, but Sid was. Sid was the driver of a lorry provided by a contractor to fetch and carry equipment and building materials to and from RAF stations. Sid left Manston one evening in 1940 to drive home in his lorry. His home was on the other side of Canterbury. Sid's headlights were almost completely blacked out but not too faint to fail to pick up the dim figure of what he took to be 'an RAF bloke' – complete with flying boots and apparently wanting a lift. Sid offered to give him a ride and the man climbed into the driving cabin. It was then that memory stirred and Sid recalled those coloured posters put up to help people to identify enemy soldiers, sailors and airmen, should invasion come. ''Ere' said Sid rather breathlessly, 'you're a f.....g Jerry, ain't yer?'

'That's right' said this young man of Goering's air force politely and added 'I suppose you had better take me to the nearest police station.' This in an impeccable public school accent.

'Well, bugger me,' said Sid and then he saw the vicious black pistol strapped to his passenger's side and he said politely, 'Would you mind giving me that thing?' The enemy answered as courteously 'Not at all' and handed Sid his pistol. Then as Sid started up his engine again the Luftwaffe pilot, who had been brought down nearby and for whom the countryside was then being scoured, said 'Look here, you know, I don't want to take you out of your way: if you go about a mile up this road, turn left by the pub, approximately a hundred yards further on, just short of the church, you'll find the local constable's house – he'll do.' Sid stared ahead – 'shook' as they used to say 'rigid', as he reflected on the amazing Intelligence of the enemy.

Then he ventured ''ow do you know sir?' – the 'sir' seemed to come naturally. 'Oh, I was at school at Canterbury. We used to come here scrumping apples and one day the bobby collared us and took us to his cottage for a telling-off.'

An American GI on leave in London was as brusque in his demand for surrender as the Brigadier in Bastogne had been with his reply. He obtained unconditional surrender in the following exchange:

GI – 'Say I am a man of few words – yes or no?'
Girl – 'Boy, you certainly talked me into it.'

If surrender is simply not 'on' it is the soldier's duty to 'sell his life'. Apropos this phrase – a not so well-known piece of Churchilliana was the great man's reply to a friend telling him that royalties from the sale of Field Marshal Montgomery's memoirs were reputed to have reached £200,000. 'Well, he acted in the best traditions of the army didn't he?', observed Winston: 'He sold his life dearly.'

"...I DON'T WANT TO TAKE YOU OUT OF YOUR WAY.."
"....NEVER PRACTISED THE MANOEUVRE IN PEACE...."
"...I AM NON-COMBATANT, IN ARTIRRERY..."
"YES OR NO?"

# XV. BLESS 'EM ALL.

Here finally is an assortment of clangs from bells which did not strike a suitable note for inclusion in the preceding chimes. We will start with the theme of the song popular with the army in the last war 'There'll be no promotion this side of the ocean, so cheer up my lads, bless 'em all.' It certainly seemed so in Home Forces, but some members of the RAF could not complain.

After Dunkirk orders were issued to the effect that all flying personnel were to be promoted to NCO; whereas a man could at that time have flown operationally as an aircraftsman he was now immediately promoted to sergeant. The new regulations did not go down well with long service non-flying technical types who had been in from peace-time days – nor with the long-serving, slowly promoted corporals and sergeants – even erks!

One of the new sergeants was waiting in the Guard Room to report out on a forty-eight hour pass, wearing his 'whiter than white' three stripes, when an aircraftsman ground crew, who was almost old enough to be his father, poked his head in and asked 'Is there a sergeant around?' The air-gunner drew himself up and said 'I am a sergeant!' 'Nah' the old erk dismissed him with a glance. 'I mean a *real* sergeant!'

Of course to his mind 'real' sergeants had to be substantive, temporary promotion did not count any more than it did in the Guardsman's lament, Roll on my three. (We make corporals by the score, let 'em reign a week or more, bust 'em down make up some more – roll on my three.) Of course progress along the road to promotion may be accelerated by catching the eye of suitably placed high personages. A certain senior member of General Wavell's staff when he was a divisional commander at

Aldershot before the war used, when in camp, to do physical exercises in the morning outside his tent, which happened to be next to the General's. (Happy accident or crafty planning?) This performance earned the sardonic comment from the batman of the General's ADC (Brian Fergusson), 'See yon feller doing his exercises in front of the General's tent? Sweatin' on promotion I call it.'

For every man sweating on promotion there may be one sweating on demotion. During the time that Monty and Eisenhower were not hitting it off too well together the King received the latter to dinner. After the meal he asked 'Ike' for his opinion of the British leader. 'Ike' said that he had a great admiration for Monty – for his remarkable tactical talents and so on, – 'But', he was moved to say lugubriously, 'I always feel that he's after my job'. His Majesty smiled gently and said, 'That's rather comforting, I sometimes think that he is after mine!'

Admiral Lord Jervis, a century ago, observed that discipline could be summed up in one word 'Obedience'. A 'their's is not to reason why' approach probably very suitable to the material he had to deal with and one that would have been appreciated by the young lance corporal plaintively complaining of his squad of recruits, 'If they'd *do* what they're told, they'd be told what to do.'

To ensure that 'sprogs', 'rookies' and even old soldiers at times, do do what they are told Service Police exist. The traditional scorn and dislike of any Servicemen for their police can remain long after they leave the service. Three army veterans were sitting in their local over pints and talking of old times. One had been a 'Red cap' and was trying to convince his old acquaintances that the Military Police were not as black as his mates painted them; that they were as effective in war, in their own way, as any other Corps. 'After all' he wound up, 'the RMPs suffered more casualties, in proportion, than any other lot.'

'Well, that's natural enough' said one of his drinking pals taking a final swig from his tankard as he got up to leave, '*they* had two bloody enemies – them *and* us!'

The name of Blackpool, Lancs doesn't figure on any Regimental or Squadron standard as a battle honour – nevertheless it *was* a notorious battlefield. The town was already established as an RAF billeting and training area for future flying types and also for those destined to help them into the air and get them down safely – when, with the fall of France, there arrived a horde of Poles, Czechs and what have you along with a large number of disgruntled soldiery who, to a man, considered that the RAF had let them down at Dunkirk. These last were liable to haul off and belt any erk at the drop of a handkerchief. The only time they considered themselves any national kin of the RAF was when a man of either service was involved in a fracas with those Poles and Czechs who, with their 'bloody heel-clicking' and Continental courtesies, appealed to the Lancashire lasses no end. Thus in those places of entertainment where servicemen foregathered the atmosphere had much the same low flash-point as that of 100 high-octane aircraft fuel and the town as a whole – on pay-nights, bore the same sober, stable aspect as that of a wide open Yukon boom-town during the Gold Rush. The Service Police – Military and RAF, were kept very busy.

A certain very large SP corporal was prominent around the town's trouble spots and he was always accompanied by another who was, for a Service Policeman, undersized. When he was asked why he always chose the little fellow to accompany him the big fellow explained, 'Look, when we go in somewhere to break up a scrap, who do you think they hit first? 'Im or me.'

The Special Branches of the Service Police deal with the more serious crime of the Sherlock Holmes type such as, for example, forgery or theft; not of course just scrounging. Scrounging has been defined as getting illegally what you are entitled to – quite different from 'liberating' which was basically thieving.

At one RAF station there had been rather too much liberating of service fuel for the running of privately-owned cars and the CO of a fighter squadron gathered everyone outside at 'B' Flight dispersal for a talking to. He did it very well with 'I have had reports that personnel of the squadron are filching service petrol – not merely motor transport fuel but also the very essential aircraft petrol – for joy riding in their cars and on their motor bikes. If at any time henceforth such theft comes to my notice, whoever and I mean *whoever* is guilty, he will be punished very severely indeed.'

All were respectfully silent. 'Dad' had spoken. One of his flight leaders stepped forward to dismiss the parade but the CO stopped him with 'Just a minute Jimmy' and he turned again to the assembled airmen and said with a straight face, 'If any of you happen to have any spare petrol coupons I'd be happy to discuss a reasonable price for them'.

In defence of drill pigs' obtuseness the great variety of types he had to deal with was quoted as a mitigating circumstance.

An American General is supposed to have summed up the variety of types under his command more concisely, 'My boys' he said, 'are like abunch of bananas; some are green, some are yellow and some are plumb rotten'.

At least not many drill pigs, if any, had to face the problems that the incorporation of the WRNS, WRAC and WAAF into the armed forces brought. Some of the problems were strictly personal. One recruit to the (then) ATS in 1939 has testified that their drill sergeant had difficulty in deciding 'whether he should dress us by our feet or our bosoms'. A problem that the greatest Bosom of them all, RSM Brand, must have been thankful he did not have to face.

It is not only on the 'square' that the instructor is tried to the limit. In 1916 – and twenty-five years later it would probably have been as true – an instructor in battle drills, in this case bayonet fighting, was approached by one of *his* bunch of bananas. 'Excuse me, sergeant, but have the Germans the same methods in bayonet fighting as we have?' The sergeant replied, 'Let's hope so, it's your only chance.'

Training, of course, can be as tedious for the trainee as for the trainer – just look at those bored stiff, sleepy old lions in a circus! After the war exercises in BAOR were incessant and not always too well conducted or instructive. After one such, at the de-briefing, the then CO of the Queens was asked for his comments. He rose in the crowded hall, almost as sacred a place of worship of Mars as the Rawlinson Hall at the Staff College and proclaimed 'The bigger the exercise, the bigger the balls-up; this is the biggest exercise I have ever been on'. Amid a flabbergasted silence he sat down. There was little doubt that he was right, but he was wrong to say so! He was passed over for promotion but received accelerated transfer to 'civvy street' – and with no golden bowler as a consolation either!

The bowler hat and rolled umbrella has for many ages been the uniform of the Whitehall Warriors and their ilk but Phylis Dixie brought a different 'undress' uniform to the Whitehall Theatre and introduced a cult that has thrived since. It has been the custom of servicemen to collect pin-ups since time immemorial but usually they were discreetly hidden away in the man's 'locker' or its equivalent. One CO was a bit of a prude. He didn't much care for his pilots pasting pin-ups all over the hut walls although the pin-ups of the war years were pretty innocuous compared with the present day nothing-left-to imagination efforts in the 'girlie magazines'. Most of them were culled from 'Men Only', then a pocket-size magazine which contained quite respectable nudes, any one of whom might have been a vicar's daughter gone only a little astray. Nevertheless the CO would periodically tell his pilots to 'Get that rubbish off the wall'.

One day 'Father' entered 'A' Flight hut and after a chat on operations in general his eye fell on a large glossy photograph of a gorgeous Betty Grable type blonde wearing very little. An affectionate greeting and signature was scrawled in the right bottom corner. 'Whose is that?' growled the CO. 'It's mine sir,' admitted a very young, pink-faced newcomer to the squadron. 'I know you have not been with us long' said 'Father', 'but you should know by now that I think that sort of trash lowers the tone of a squadron establishment. Photos of relatives and friends is one thing but ..... *that*, I don't like it.'

'But sir' ventured the new boy brightly, 'that's my mother.'

He escaped a severe reprimand because it was *true.* His father's second wife, well-known in the West End, was what is now known as a stripper.

In the old days, when discipline ruled the land and a murderer, instead of receiving a scolding from a psychiatrist, paid for his crime with his life, and it was customary for newspaper reporters to write that 'the condemned man ate a hearty breakfast'. Hearty in one sense it may have been but scarcely hilarious. Without the same excuse breakfast in an Officers Mess was often a pretty grim and silent affair, taken in an atmosphere of impending doom – perhaps the senior major was about to explode, and that would be in the megaton range! But on one occasion a Mess Sergeant *did* provide an appropriate reason for a deathly hush. He entered the room, approached the Adjutant, and without showing any more concern than if he was announcing that the milk had gone off, informed him that 'There's a man hanged himself in the lavatory sir.'

All good things – and bad, they say, come to an end and whereas some duration-of-war-only soldiers, sailors and airmen viewed their getting out with hilarious relief, others regarded their demob' with dark foreboding about the pitfalls awaiting them in 'civvy street'. Some were better equipped than others to cope with the complications of civilian life. While they were in the services some had loathed every moment – others had never had it so good.

Two airmen, soon to be civilians, met at the Uxbridge demobilisation centre where they were to collect their civilian clothes presented to them by a grateful RAF. One was a young squadron-leader – the other was a leading-aircraftsman – the former had been an 'intrepid bird-man', the latter an airframe fitter on the same squadron and while the squadron-leader had originally joined up while still at university, the LAC had been able to put in several very useful, though hard, pre-war years' experience of the cut and thrust of 'civvy street' in the purlieus of the Elephant and Castle. As they shared decisions about ties, socks, shoes, suits and shirts in a Nissen hut, which looked like a temporary 'Marks an' Sparks', they arranged to have a farewell beer or two before they stepped out of the 'Airworks' for ever. They emerged from the Centre still in uniform and carrying their cardboard cartons of civilian clothes – the squadron-leader had one carton – the LAC had two. The squadron-leader was afoot – the LAC had what he called his 'lardy' (lardy-dah-car) in the shape of a quite respectable-looking Ford 8 saloon. The LAC stopped the car outside Uxbridge Underground station saying he was going to get 'some ackers to buy our drinks'. Instead of going into a bank or post office for his 'ackers' however, he went into the railway station carrying one of his two cartons – this puzzled the squadron-leader waiting in the Ford.

The LAC came out fifteen minutes later and, with a broad wink, started the car and drove to a big pub on the town's outskirts. Over an extended lunch-hour booze-up he told his companion that all, including a lunch to follow, was 'on' him because of a deal he'd made. Back at their squadron he'd got wind of a current racket organised by what were then known as spivs. These 'fly-boys' haunted railway stations and bus stops near demob' centres offering, in these days of clothing coupons and rationing, to pay cash to gullible servicemen for their cartons full of civvy clothes. There'd be a sidling approach, a flashing of bank notes and a quick passing over of cartons by the many demobbed bods. 'Seven quid I got from that sly bleeder', said the LAC smugly. The squadron-leader, who himself had few enough civilian clothes, having joined up when only a couple of years out of school and worn only uniform since, wasn't sure of the deal. 'But surely you'll need those clothes' he said. – 'Not me cock,' the LAC assured him with his new-found freedom of speech to an almost quondam officer. 'They wasn't sharp enough for me – I'll sell them and get mine dahn the Boro.' 'But you've sold them' said the other. 'Nah,' the ex-fitter grinned at him, 'y'see, I got a spare cardboard box and some string from a geezer back at the Centre and filled it up while I waited for you in the motor and all that bloody spiv at the station got for 'is seven quid was my old 'angar overalls, a pair o' long flannel underpants with the arse out of 'em, a wore-out pair of wellingtons, two dirty shirts, all tore, six pairs o' stinkin' socks and my old workin' tunic – smuvvered wiv f.....g oil – 'anded over sight unseen as they say.'

Thus the last clanger in our collection of clangers was dropped by a civvy.

WAY OUT
CIVVY ST

"BLESS
HQ

'EM ALL"
S/LR PETE
RAF
SP

# THE PASSING OF PILOT OFFICER PRUNE
## by Bill Hooper

Any passing of Percy Prune created havoc for those in the vicinity. As the legendary fool, mug, clot and affable dim-wit of the war-time RAF, he 'served' as the awful example of what not to do in the air. And yet he was beloved, not only by RAF and Commonwealth airmen but also by those of the Free French, American and other Allied Air Forces. Cartoons of Prune were found on the walls of Russian pilots' messes and even 'The Enemy' had a soft spot for him – 'Someone' in the Goering's Luftwaffe actually 'awarded' him the Iron Cross 'For having destroyed so many Allied aircraft'.

A fool is funny whatever his vintage – Bertie Wooster tickles the moderns as much as 'Brother' in the person of Derek Nimmo. Prune is still laughed at in the student chambers of Cambridge, in the messes of the modern RAF and Commonwealth pilots, as well as in the clubs and pubs of those who knew him, and accounts of his doings are still asked for by editors in Canada and Australia – as well as by television producers 'at home'.

This has encouraged his cartoon-creator to set down the hitherto unpublished life story of Percy Prune – his birth at Ineyne, his schooldays at St Finga's, Herts, his brief university career at St Clewelesse College, Cambridge, his service days and ultimate retirement to Sussex. The author repeats the fact that 'There's a little bit of Prune in all of us' while Prune, himself, adds 'And if the cap fits it won't fall over deaf ears'.

Published by

MIDAS BOOKS

12 Dene Way, Speldhurst,
Tunbridge Wells, Kent TN3 0NX

ISBN 0 85936 025 3